ENDORSEMENTS

"With heart and soul, passion and technique, Chris McNulty has answered the question many students have asked of me, 'Darryl, can you teach me how to scat? Improvise? Sing?' This book is a comprehensive stepwise approach that will prove invaluable in the development of today's singers. I have longed for a pedagogy this rich. Brilliantly structured and clearly presented in her sophisticated yet accessible methodology, VCM will be required reading for those students who ask, the few who don't, as well as the ones who are acrobatically riffing and running through a handful of cliched pop melismas. Thank you, Chris. Young singers in search of a voice need this book. You are the *compleat* musician!"

    Darryl Tookes
    Composer, singer, pianist, educator,
    Tisch School of the Arts, NYU; Purchase College, SUNY

"A most concise, well structured, and easy to understand book for all vocalists (and instrumentalists!) who want to become versatile, have more confidence, and be better overall musicians. Chris McNulty's *Vocalist As Complete Musician* is a comprehensive and engaging method designed to help you hear, sing, and play music on a deeper level. Practicing these exercises WILL really enhance HOW you hear, sing, and play music!"

    Dena DeRose
    Jazz Vocalist and Pianist, Jazz Voice Professor at the University of Music and Performing Arts, Graz, Austria

"If Chris McNulty's singing, both live and recorded, is any reflection of her own expertise on the tetrachord method of improvisation, then this book can help you and your students, too! Chris is a world class jazz singer, and this is priceless musical instruction for any singer who wants to infuse their singing with improvisation, whether re-melodizing a song with lyrics, or scat singing. Brava Chris!"

    Amy London
    Jazz Vocalist and Educator. Motema recording artist
    Jazz Faculty, New School, City College; Hofstra University; Jazz House, Mannes Prep, New York and jazz camps worldwide

"With the publication of *Vocalist As Complete Musician: Utilizing Tetrachords,* Chris has generously shared the personal methodology that has enabled her to develop a unique style and solid musicianship. If you systematically study this book, which will take time and effort, you can eventually put the materials together in your own way, which is what every great jazz musician has done throughout time. Thank you dear Chris, for giving us the opportunity to expand our ears and mind and to find note choices and colors that we hadn't previously thought of!!!"

Suzanne Pittson
Vocalist, Pianist, Educator
Assistant Professor of Jazz Vocal Studies, The City College of New York

"Congratulations to Chris McNulty on this fantastic book. An innovative, practical method for vocalists (and other instrumentalists) to develop their improvising skills, from the perspective of a great jazz vocalist."

Nick Haywood
Jazz musician, Senior Lecturer, Conservatorium of Music,
University of Tasmania

"*Vocalist as Complete Musician* opens singers ears with a fresh new method of ear training, opening up a palette of new note choices, you'll actually 'Hear and Use'. Practicing licks and scales without using them over a song doesn't stick. Chris McNulty's tetra chord method guides you through a song using all the harmonies you'll ever want to hear!"

Roseanna Vitro
Grammy Nominated Jazz Singer, Educator and Journalist

Vocalist as Complete Musician

UTILIZING TETRACHORDS

Chris McNulty

McNulty Music | Australia

Published in Australia by
McNulty Music
email: mcnultyjazz@gmail.com
website: www.chrismcnulty.com

First published in Australia 2017
2nd Edition June 2020
Copyright © Chris McNulty 2017

All rights reserved. No part of this publication may be reproduced, stored in a retrieval system, or transmitted, in any form or by any means without the prior written permission of the publisher, nor be otherwise circulated in any form of binding or cover other than that in which it is published and without a similar condition being imposed on the subsequent purchaser.

McNulty, Chris
VOCALIST AS COMPLETE MUSICIAN: Utilizing Tetrachords

ISBN: 978-164136919-0

Cover layout and design by Dmitry Kulayev
Sibelius files and pdf layout by Chris McNulty
Final layout and proof reading by Wade Gregory
Proof reading and content review by Nick Haywood
Audio duo tracks #1-8, #11, #14, #17, #18 by David J. Allardice
Duo tracks mixed and engineered by David J. Allardice, Frog Hollow Studios, Hartwell, Vic, Australia
Audio trio tracks: #9, 10, #12, #13, #15, #16 - Ben Matthews, Alistair Peel
Trio tracks engineered by Brodie Stewart at Brodie Stewart Studios, Mt, Lawley, Perth, WA
Trio tracks mixed and Mastered by Dave Darlington, Bass Hit Studios, NYC, NY
All vocal tracks by Chris McNulty
Front cover photography by Mandarine Montgomery
Back cover photography by Angeline Wolfe

Disclaimer
All care has been taken in the preparation of the information herein, but no responsibility can be accepted by the publisher or author for any damages resulting from the misinterpretation of this work. All contact details given in this book were current at the time of publication, but are subject to change.

The advice given in this book is based on the experience of the individuals. Professionals should be consulted for individual problems. The author and publisher shall not be responsible for any person with regard to any loss or damage caused directly or indirectly by the information in this book.

DOWNLOADING YOUR AUDIO TRACKS

There are 22 tracks accompanying Exercises 1 through 11c

Please visit or click on the following URL

https://chrismcnulty.com/VCMAUDIOTRACKS

or go to

www.chrismcnulty.com/vcm-the-book

and click on the **Download Audio** button

The MP3's have been created at either 320 kbps or 192 kbps

Sibelius files for Ex 9b and 10a, 10b & 10c are available for those who have the program. You may find these useful for your students as these are manipulable. Please check the VCM page at the above web site address for further details.

I would also like to ask out of respect to us as vocal musicians and educators, that you refrain from file sharing pdf's or mp3 tracks. We have to trust in your integrity and hope you will honor this request. Thank you.

ABOUT THE AUTHOR

Australian-American jazz vocalist-composer, Chris McNulty moved to the United States in 1988 and has been a fixture on the New York jazz scene for almost three decades. Her seven album releases in the USA have received wide critical acclaim including her latest album, *Eternal*, a chamber ensemble and jazz quintet collaboration with orchestrator, Steve Newcomb and pianist-arranger, John Di Martino which placed #11 on the 80th DownBeat Readers Poll in 2015 for Album of the Year.

McNulty has performed throughout Russia, the UK, Ireland, Europe, the Middle East, Central America and Lebanon including festival appearances at the Edinburgh Jazz Festival, Kilkenny Arts Fest (Ireland), Breckon Jazz Fest (Wales), Kharkov Jazz Fest (Ukraine), White Nights Jazz Fest, St Petersburg (Russia) and Petrozavodsk Jazz Fest (Russia) as well as the Perth, Wangaratta and Melbourne International Jazz Festivals in Australia. Among the jazz greats she has performed and recorded with are the late pianists Mulgrew Miller and John Hicks, saxophonists Gary Bartz, Gary Thomas, David Pietro, Frank Wess, Tineke Postma and Joel Frahm, drummers Billy Hart, Matt Wilson, Tony Reedus, Montez Coleman and Marcus Gilmore, Trumpeter Ingrid Jensen and her long time colleagues, bassist Ugonna Okegwo and guitarist Paul Bollenback.

The American magazine Jazz Times has described her vocalizing as "fearless" and her composing as "peerless." Britain's Jazz Wise magazine describes her as possessing "a voice of serene beauty, striking veracity and compelling emotional fervency."

In 2013 Chris was the recipient of the Australian Jazz Bell award for the Best Australian Jazz Vocal Album for her album *The Song That Sings You Here*. Since relocating back to Melbourne in early 2016 she has performed at the Perth International Jazz Festival, Stonnington Jazz Festival and the Wangaratta International Festival of Jazz and Blues and most recently at the invitation of the National Gallery of Victoria and MIJF for their MoMA jazz series.

In December 2018 the 2019 Bundanon Trust Prelude Composer Residency awards were announced. McNulty was among the six Australian composers selected. She is currently completing her year long residency at Gallop House in Perth, WA. *Vocalist As Complete Musician* - **VCM** is McNulty's first educational publication. She continues to tour internationally.

ACKNOWLEDGMENTS

Enormous gratitude to Michelle Picker for her expertise, support and guidance and for the digital platform set up and art work review. Special thanks to David J. Allardice for his expertise, time and patience in engineering and creating the duo audio tracks. Ben Matthews and Alistar Peel for their musical contributions and Brodie Stewart for his fine engineering and keen ears on the trio tracks. The amazing as always, Dave Darlington in NYC for mixing and mastering the trio tracks. Nick Haywood for his excellent proofreading of text, editing suggestions and generosity. Wade Gregory for providing the final polish of layout, systemizing and reviewing of my Sibelius files and the excellent proofreading of my music notation. Dmitry Kulayev for his diligence and awesome cover art design and last but not least, the amazing Bob Stoloff for his wonderful foreword, extraordinary humor and tremendous encouragement.

Thank you to all my dear friends and colleagues around the world for your continued support and friendship. I'm especially grateful to my Australian friends: Belinda (Bluey) Madden, Daylene and Billy Tomasini, Yvonne Kuehne, Sonia Barreto and Pierrick Hovette, Geoff Cheung, Paula De Burgh and the late Shane Hughes, Helen Morse, Cher Fay, Gaye Lyons, Steve Newcomb, Miriam Zolin, Timo Juntunen, Angeline Wolfe, Georgie Dawson and Nick Buskens, Marguerite Grey and Aussie vocalist/musicians — Clancye Milne, Penny King, Bronwyn Sprogowski, Margaret Morrison, Brigid O'Donohue, Anita Wardell and Carl Mackey. In the USA: I'd like to especially thank Darryl Tookes, Dena DeRose, Roseanna Vitro, Suzanne Pittson, Jay Clayton, Amy London, Sarah James, Janis Wilkins, Holli Ross, Fay Victor, Jane Irving, Tessa Souter, Roz Corral, Sheila Jordan, John Di Martino, Nancy and Geoff Pitcher and Ann Braithwaite.

A special thank you to guitarist, educator Paul Bollenback for introducing me to this fabulous tool — the Tetrachord.

© Chris McNulty 2017

Dedicated to

Mark Murphy, Graham Wood and Sam McNulty

TABLE OF CONTENTS

1. Foreword
2. Introduction
3. Before We Dig In!

Chapter One — Working with the Basic Tetrachord and Scale template
5. Ex.1 Getting Started: Singing and integrating tetrachords (track 1)

Chapter Two — The Major Scale — For Beginner Students
7. Ex.2 The Major scale (track 2)

Chapter Three — The Melodic Minor Scale — Intermediate/advanced
11. The Melodic Minor scale
13. Ex.3 Melodic Minor scale-chord uses (track 3)
17. The Harmonic Minor scale
19. Ex.4 Harmonic Minor scale scale-chord uses (track 4)
23. Ex.5a. Extra drilling over Altered Scale (track 5)
27. Ex.5b Alternating between the Altered Scale and the Diminished (Half-whole)
29. Ex.5c Extra drilling over Arabic Scale (track 6)

Chapter Four — The Diminished Scale
33. Ex.6 Diminished Scale use over Dom 7 chords (track 7)
41. Ex.7 Diminished Scale use over Diminished 7 chords (track 8)

Chapter Five — Singing tetrachords over harmony using one root for each key
47. Ex.8 Getting used to singing the tetrachord shapes over specific chord changes (tracks 9, 10)

Chapter Six — Singing scales using tetrachords over II, V, I, VI progression
58. Ex.9a Preparation: Singing the tetrachords over the first progression (starting in the key of C) (track 11)
62. Ex.9b Singing scales using tetrachords over II, V, I, VI progression through all 12 keys (tracks 12, 13)

© Chris McNulty 2017

Chapter Seven — **Hearing and Soloing over a specific set of chord changes**
    81.   Ex.10a Warming up over scale/chords (track 14)
    86.   Ex.10b Preparation for singing over the changes of "Softly" (track 16)
    92.   Ex.10c Using the method to improvise over "Softly (tracks 15 & 16)

Chapter Eight — **Pentatonic Chord-Scale uses** — **Major and Minor**
    95.   Ex.11a Pentatonic scale use exercise (major & minor) (track 17)
    97.   Ex.11b Pentatonic scale use over Chris' New Day vamp (track 18)

Appendices — **Chord-Scale Source Templates**
    102. Appendix 1. Chord-Scale tetrachord structures
    105. Appendix 2. Chord-Scale relationships (Parallel & Derivative uses)
    107. Appendix 3. Types of Dom 7 chord qualities, short cuts and scale choices
    108. Appendix 4. Common tone-chord/scale relationships
    111. Appendix 5. Chord voicing short cuts
    113. Appendix 6. Interchangeable chord options (what you see / what you can play)
    114. Appendix 7. The pentatonic scale
    115. Appendix 8. BeBop scale uses (a) chart (b) exercise
    117. Appendix 9. Whole Tone scale uses

Audio Track listings — (pg. 118)
    Tracks 1-8, 11, 14, 17, 18 **with piano and voice**
    Tracks 9-10, 12-13, 15-16 **with trio**

Glossary — **Explanation of terms used throughout this book** (pg. 119)

Music Fundamentals for Beginners (pg. 121)

© Chris McNulty 2017

FOREWORD

It never even occurred to me to learn via tetrachords as I grew up in the old school of octave bookend scales and pattern permutations. But this makes much more sense particularly for vocalists who are already quite used to using tetrachords as warm up exercises. The design and intent are both excellent. Chris has done a terrific job integrating the essentials of theory, ear training, harmony, composition, arranging and improvisation in one comprehensive text. It's like taking a core music course that has everything you need to become a well-rounded, versatile musician.

I also like how Chris strokes the piano as a blessed tool for all musicians. That is one instrument I wish I had stuck with as a kid. So kudos for pushing that point because as we know it makes a significant difference.

In addition to the musical elements, Chris give other aspects of performance the attention it deserves. Many books do not offer the TLC that vocalists often need. Playing an internal instrument (as opposed to one with external triggers) has, in my opinion, more personal, physical and emotional demands. Chris' visual-aural teaching approach is not only learner-friendly but is presented in such a way to encourage confidence, independence and empowerment.

I like the way she underscores the "nitty-gritty" elements of the book with a more intimate vocabulary that convert some of the more technical terms to nuances like sounds, shapes, colors and intentions. This unilateral teaching approach offers alternate diets to right and left brained folks who are struggling to understand the various dimensions of music. Most books (like mine) remain in the technical realm but Chris' MO of explanation is much more sympathetic to all levels of proficiency and personal mindsets.

So what else can I say? Chris has a great book here, and I know many singers will appreciate her expertise.

Bob Stoloff
Jazz voice and instrumental educator

© Chris McNulty 2017

INTRODUCTION

Discovering the **"Tetrachord"** has had a significant impact on my learning and teaching as a vocal jazz educator. In fact I've found it to be a really effective tool in addressing all three components of study — theory, ear training and improvisation. This book explores its uses in hearing and integrating scales along with the chords that source to them in much of what we know as "jazz harmony." By working through these exercises students and/or professional will gain a more thorough understanding of the interconnectedness between scales and chords, while helping identify both visually and aurally by sight and by ear how to improvise with more confidence and accuracy. I have also included a number of Appendix documents which I encourage readers to utilize throughout this work and hopefully beyond.

While the main focus of the book is to expand your hearing and understanding of jazz harmony, the work also provides a more complete theoretical template to develop your compositional and arranging skills. While some of you may have substantial theory under your belt others will not.

In order to have complete mastery as an improvisor one must be able to integrate both the aural and visual landscape. These are our road maps for navigating our way through harmony. Wherever possible I've created exercises in all 12 keys. I encourage working in as many keys as possible and making friends with the piano.

Outside of enhancing your knowledge of theory and improving musicianship and improvising skills, I believe that if vocalists do a little of this work every day, they're going to keep their instruments, ears and most importantly their PITCH in shape, especially throughout those lean times. So many vocalists struggle to get enough play time in between gigs. I hope using these exercises will help solve some of those issues and benefit professionals and students alike in helping to stay in "ear" and "musical stamina" shape!

I've purposely left out working on the Blues and BeBop scales other than to include a template in the Appendices. **Bob Stoloff** (*Scat*)*,* **Judy Niemack** (*Hear it, Sing it!*) and **Dan Greenblatt** (*The Blues Scales*) are all tremendously informative on these subjects.

Before We Dig In!

Let's start by defining what a "**Tetrachord**" is and what it isn't. A tetrachord is a 4 note scalar fragment. It is NOT a scale. Throughout this book we'll be using **SIX Tetrachords** only [*see Chapter One, Ex 1 - "Basic Tetrachord Template"*].

- **Major**
- **Minor I** (*dorian*)
- **Minor II** (*phrygian*)
- **Diminished**
- **Harmonic**
- **Whole tone** (*lydian*)

All six tetrachords above are found inside the following scales we'll be working (with exception of the Pentatonic scale):

- **Major**
- **Melodic Minor**
- **Harmonic Minor**
- **Diminished (1/2-whole)**
- **Diminished (Whole-1/2)**
- **Whole tone**

You will learn to recognize all six "tetrachords" in just about everything that's written and heard throughout this book.

You may have noticed that each tetrachord's name mirrors a scale name. In all cases it's because the quality of that particular tetrachord appears in the first 4 notes of any one of the scales listed above. With the exception of the Pentatonic scale all the scales we'll be working with are "bookended" by two tetrachords. They are either duplicates (e.g., Major, Major) OR a combination of two different tetrachords. The focus throughout this book will be on learning how to hear and use a combination of these six tetrachords to sing a myriad of scales. These source to the majority of chords we'll be using and more importantly, help you identify and hear across a myriad of simple to more complex harmonic passages. It will also help explain much of the theory behind the scales and chords we'll be investigating.

© Chris McNulty 2017

The names once again for the six tetrachords are:

Major, **Minor I** (*dorian*), **Minor II** (*phrygian*), **Whole tone** (*lydian*), **Harmonic** and **Diminished**.

In this book, with the exception of the **Harmonic Minor scale** you will only find these six tetrachords [*see explanation for non-occurring tetrachords Harmonic Minor - Chapter 3, page 19*]

Take the time to look at each piece of information or event on the stave. Give yourself time to internalize the simpler material first before moving onto the more complex exercises. Go slowly. Start from Chapter One and work though to Chapter Four. Then stay there for a while. Pick one chord from two scales and practice integrating them. Then move on to the next.

The introduction of **Parallel** and **Derivative** scale use can be a little tricky to grasp straight away. Don't worry about absorbing it all immediately. Continue to work slowly through to the end of Chapter Three. Hopefully by Chapter Four when we introduce singing over chord progressions you'll have developed a better understanding or at least grasped the difference between Parallel and Derivative use and their alternating functions [*refer to Appendix 2 for further drilling*].

I've found most of this work is best played at the piano. Even if you're not proficient you will hear much of why some things work and others don't. Always keep in mind that not all that's written or logical on paper works aurally. Theory was never meant to dictate what sounds great but to provide a resource template to the big picture. Ultimately we do this work to extend, widen our sonic landscape as well as provide us with the tools that lead to greater independence and empowerment. After your study work is done, trust your ears. The ear always overrides theory. This series of templates has been created to assist students understand where certain scales and chords are derived from and then HEAR them. To integrate the theory for practice whenever possible I've included all 12 keys. Even though I've provided tracks to every exercise to sing along with, I hope you'll make friends with the piano. It will not only make you a better and more proficient musician, you'll hear more deeply and become a better composer and arranger.

Chapter One — Working with the Basic Tetrachord Template

In order to be able to sing through the scales used in this book you will first need to integrate the sounds and shapes of each of the 6 tetrachords. The first template you'll be using is the **Basic Tetrachord template**. This is a simple drill exercise to help prepare you for the work you'll be doing on scales, so take your time to learn the sounds and shapes of each tetrachord as all six occur in just about every exercise in this book (except for the Pentatonic and Bebop scales). Make friends with them. You'll be very happy once you have because they're going to help you sing through difficult scales and harmonic passages with ease. They will also help demystify and simplify much of what's often seemed complex and confusing.

Here are the six tetrachords you'll be using throughout this book. As you will soon hear and see they're the nuts and bolts of most of the scales, shapes and sounds you'll be hearing throughout this book. They'll be your constant companion and the glue that connects the dots for sourcing a myriad of scales and chords

Throughout this book the term *"bookend"* will apply to the two tetrachords which outline or make up the sound of any particular scale you will be working with — from the first to the last note. The **"bookend"** delineates the first 4 notes and the last 4 notes of the scale. For the purpose of keeping things simple the source templates are all in the Key of "C."

Exercise 1 (track #1) — Getting Started: Singing and integrating the six tetrachords

Sing each of the **six tetrachords** up and then down, starting on middle C. Then focus on singing/playing a **Major** tetrachord starting on random notes at the piano. Then move to a **Minor I** (*dorian*) tetrachord and so on and so forth until you have sung through each of the six tetrachords starting on as many notes as you can. Then try switching them up. Sing a **Major** tetrachord starting from **F**. Then sing a Diminished tetrachord from **C** then a **Minor II** (*phrygian*) from **Eb** and so on and so forth. Sing these tetrachords within the limits of your range. Spend a few minutes a day on this. Do it whenever you think about it. Once you are comfortable you can sing all six on call or with ease move on to the next exercise.

© Chris McNulty 2017

1. Tetrachords

* Track # 1

Definition of a Tetrachord: A tetrachord is a 4 note scalar fragment (it is NOT a scale)

Throughout this book the following **Six Tetrachords** will be used as an integrating tool to hear through and over a myriad of scales and chords. You'll be seeing and hearing them lots!

Major

Minor I (*dorian*)

Minor II (*phrygian*)

Whole tone (*lydian*)

Harmonic

Diminished

We're using the root note of "C" for these introductory exercises
Start simply by singing each tetrachord up and then down from "C" as follows:

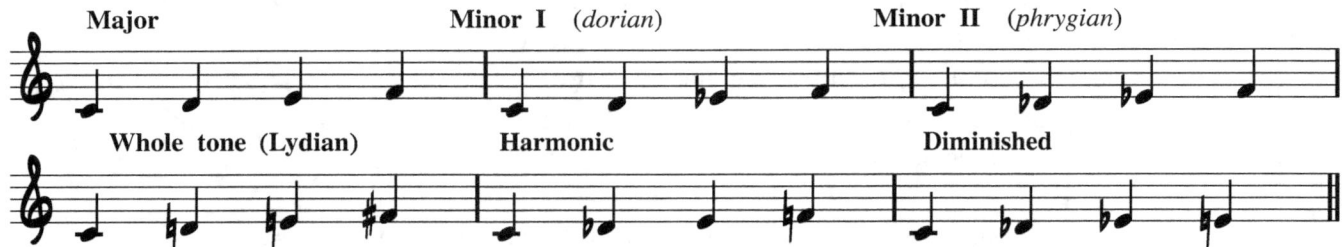

Now sing each of the six tetrachords down from "C"

At your instrument now play or sing each tetrachord from a different starting note

Sing each of them up and down starting on different notes until you feel comfortable singing each on call, starting with Major then moving through all six tetrachord shapes.

When you're comfortable pitching from any starting note move to Chapter Two (beginners) or Chapter Three (intermediate).

© Chris McNulty 2017

Chapter Two — The Major Scale — Maj 3rd, Maj 7
For Beginner students

For the purposes of getting to the nitty gritty of this method I won't be focusing much attention on the **Major** scale as I'm assuming most students have already covered this. However, I've included the scale and chords as a starting point for beginner students. **Intermediate/Advanced** students should move straight to the **Melodic Minor** scale. In all instances I've included the home scale as well as the modes and chords that source from each interval of the scale. It needs to be mentioned that these modes share the same pitches as the major scale but they are NOT the major scale — all tension points in the scales are different.

Starting from each degree of the **C Major** scale the names of the modes and their associated chords are as follows:

1st mode	— Ionian	C Maj 7
2nd mode	— Dorian	D min 7
3rd mode	— Phrygian	E min 7
4th mode	— Lydian	F Maj 7
5th mode	— Mixolydian	G Dominant 7
6th mode	— Aeolian	A min 7
7th mode	— Locrian	B 1/2 Dim

Beginner students who aren't piano proficient use the sing along tracks first with my voice and then without my voice as a guide. **Intermediate/Advanced** students once you've spent time working with the audio tracks I'd suggest doing most of these preparatory exercises at the piano. A good way to deal with this is to play the chord (root, 3rd, 7th) in the left hand using the sustain pedal. Then play/sing the bookend tetrachords which make up the scale. Hear how the scale sounds once you sing the two tetrachords back to back. Then move to the 2nd degree of the scale and repeat the process of singing bookend tetrachords up each scale degree, making sure to use the accompanying chord that sources to each degree of the scale. You'll soon hear why some of these chords and scales are used more frequently than others. Keep in mind theory is most useful when seen/used as a road map or template for explaining systems and why and how scales exist. However by hearing and recognizing aurally, we learn a lot more about why certain sounds and harmonic choices are used, not only in composition and arranging but also in improvisation.

Exercise 2 (track #2) — The Major Scale — Maj 3rd, Maj 7

Introduces the following tetrachords:

> **Major**
> **Minor I** (*dorian*)
> **Minor II** (*phrygian*)
> **Whole tone** (*lydian*)

The **1st mode** of "C" **M**ajor is **C Ionian** — **Chord: CMaj7**
The two tetrachords that bookend the Ionian scale are the same:
(1) **Major** (C, D, E, F) and (2) **Major** (G, A, B, C)

The **2nd mode** of "C" Major is **D Dorian** — **Chord: Dmin7**
The two tetrachords that bookend the Dorian scale are the same:
(1) **Minor I** (*dorian*) (D, E, F, G) and (2) **Minor I** (*dorian*) (A, B, C D)

The **3rd mode** of "C" Major is **E Phrygian** — **Chord: Emin7**
The two tetrachords that bookend the Phrygian scale are:
(1) **Minor II** (*phrygian*) (E, F, G, A) and (2) **Minor II** (*phrygian*) (B, C, D, E)

The **4th mode** of "C" Major is **F Lydian** — **Chord: F Maj 7 #11**
The two tetrachords that make up the Lydian scale differ.
The tetrachords are: (1) **Whole tone** (*lydian*) (F, G, A, B) and (2) **Major** (C, D, E, F)

The **5th mode** of "C" Major is **G Mixolydian** — **Chord: G7**
The two tetrachords that make up the Mixolydian scale differ.
The tetrachords are: (1) **Major** (G, A, B, C), (2) **Minor I** (*dorian*) (D, E, F, G)

The **6th mode** of "C" Major is **A Aeolian** — **Chord: Amin7**
The two tetrachords that make up the Aeolian scale differ.
The tetrachords are: (1) **Minor I** (*dorian*) (A, B, C, D) (2) **Minor II** (*phrygian*) (E, F, G, A)

The **7th mode** of "C" Major is **B Locrian** — **Chord: B 1/2 Dim**
The two tetrachords that make up the Locrian scale differ.
The tetrachords are: (1) **Minor II** (*phrygian*) (B, C, D, E) (2) **Whole tone** (*lydian*) (F, G, A, B)

© Chris McNulty 2017

2. The Major Scale
Using C Major scale

*Track #2

Chord: Cmaj7

Scale: Ionian (Major): Maj 3, Maj 7

Tetrachords: Major, Major

W W 1/2 W W W 1/2

Chord: Dm7

Scale: Dorian (Minor): b3, b7

Tetrachords: Minor I (*dorian*), Minor I (*dorian*)

W 1/2 W W W 1/2 W

Chord: Em7(b9)

Scale: Phrygian (Spanish Minor): b9, b3, b13, b7

Tetrachords: Minor II (*phrygian*), Minor II (*phrygian*)

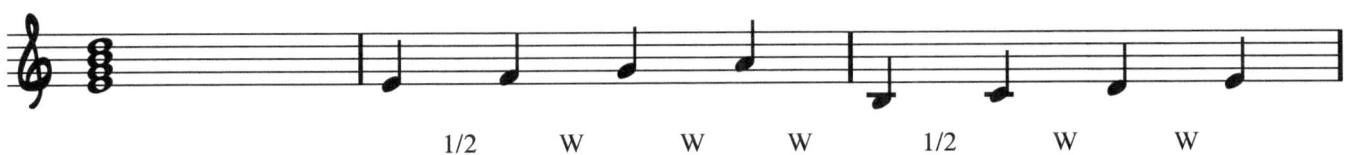

1/2 W W W 1/2 W W

Chord: Fmaj7(#11)

Scale: Lydian (Major 7 #11): #11, Maj 7

Tetrachords: Whole tone (*lydian*), Major

W W W 1/2 W W 1/2

© Chris McNulty 2017

Chord: G7

Scale: Mixolydian: (Dom 7): nat 9, nat 13, b7

Tetrachords: Major   Minor I (*dorian*)

Chord: Am7

Scale: Aeolian: (Natural/Relative Minor b13): nat 9, b3, b13, b7

Tetrachords: Minor I (*dorian*)   Minor II (*phrygian*)

Chord: Bm7(b5)

Scale: Locrian: (1/2 Diminished): b9, b3, b5, b13, b7

Tetrachords: Minor II (*phrygian*)   Whole tone (*Lydian*)

Chapter Three — The Melodic Minor Scale — Min 3rd, Maj 7th

Intermediate students

The **Melodic Minor** scale introduces us to the **Diminished Tetrachord** along with the four tetrachords already identified from the Major scale above. In this exercise we'll discover the source of some of the more colorful and interesting chords and scales used in jazz harmony. Take your time to familiarize yourself with the information I've included above and below the staves. The first thing you'll notice is the delineation of **"Parallel"** and **"Derivative"** use. **Parallel** defines the scale from the root of the chord. **Derivative** defines the scale from its **"Parent scale"** — the parent scale referenced in this exercise is the **Melodic Minor** scale. This may not make sense immediately. However, as you move through this work the difference will become clearer. Learning how it can assist you as an improvisor in analysis and choosing/hearing scale choices over chords is integral.

Obviously the first degree of **C Melodic Minor** is going to be "C Melodic minor" which is of course the parent scale. The first degree of a scale is the only instance where **Parallel** and **Derivative** are one and the same. All that changes however, once you move to the 2nd degree of the scale. You'll understand this more clearly once you start working with the tracks. In each system event (above the stave) both **Parallel** and **Derivative** uses are suggested, as well as the chord quality and its name. On each track you'll first hear the chord, the root or starting note, followed by tetrachords. We always start at the first degree of the scale then move to the 2nd degree, playing/singing the accompanying chord and tetrachord and so on and so forth. Go through this exercise either with the track or at the piano a few times a day for a week or more or until each scale degree and its accompanying chord are identified and heard (using the tetrachords I've given you) before moving on to the **Harmonic Minor** scale.

Exercise 3 (track #3) — Melodic Minor Scale (Min 3rd, Maj 7th)

The **1st mode** of "C" Melodic Minor is **C Melodic Minor**
Chord CMin-Maj 7

Tetrachords: (1) **Minor I** (*dorian*) (C, D, Eb, F) (2) **Major** (G, A, B, C)

The **2nd mode** of "C" Melodic Minor is **D Phrygian, Natural 6**
Chord: Dsus13 b9

Tetrachords: (1) **Minor II** (*phrygian*) (D, Eb, F, G) and (2) **Minor I** (*Dorian*) (A, B, C, D)   *** voice the chord as **Ebmaj7#11/D**

The **3rd mode** of "C" Melodic Minor is **E Lydian Augmented**
Chord: Eb+maj7

Tetrachords: (1) **Whole Tone** (*lydian*) (Eb, F, G, A) and (2) **Diminished** (B, C, D, Eb)

The **4th mode** of "C" Melodic Minor is **F Lydian Dominant**
Chord: F7 #11

Tetrachords: (1) **Whole tone** (*lydian*) (F, G, A, B) and (2) **Minor I** (C, D, Eb, F)

The **5th mode** of "C" Melodic Minor is **G Dominant b13**
Chord: G7b13

Tetrachords: (1) **Major** (G, A, B, C) and (2) **Minor II** (*phrygian*) (D, Eb, F, G)

The **6th mode** of "C" Melodic Minor is **A Locrian, Natural 2**
Chord: Aminb5

Tetrachords: (1) **Minor I** (*dorian*) (A, B, C, D) and (2) **Whole tone** (*Lydian*) **(Eb, F, G, A)**

The **7th mode** of "C" Melodic Minor is **B Altered** (also known as the Diminished-Whole tone scale — **Chord: B7b9 #9 #11 b13**

Tetrachords: (1) **Diminished** (B, C, D, Eb) and (2) **Whole tone (lydian)** (F, G, A, B)

3. Melodic Minor Scale
Chord-Scale uses
Using "C" Melodic Minor

1st Degree of C Melodic Minor

Chord Quality: (b3, Major 7th)

Chord: Cmi^ma7

Parallel: C Minor/Major 7 - Played from the root of the chord

Derivative: Play parent scale from root

1st mode of scale is the only instance where Parallel and Derivative are one and the same

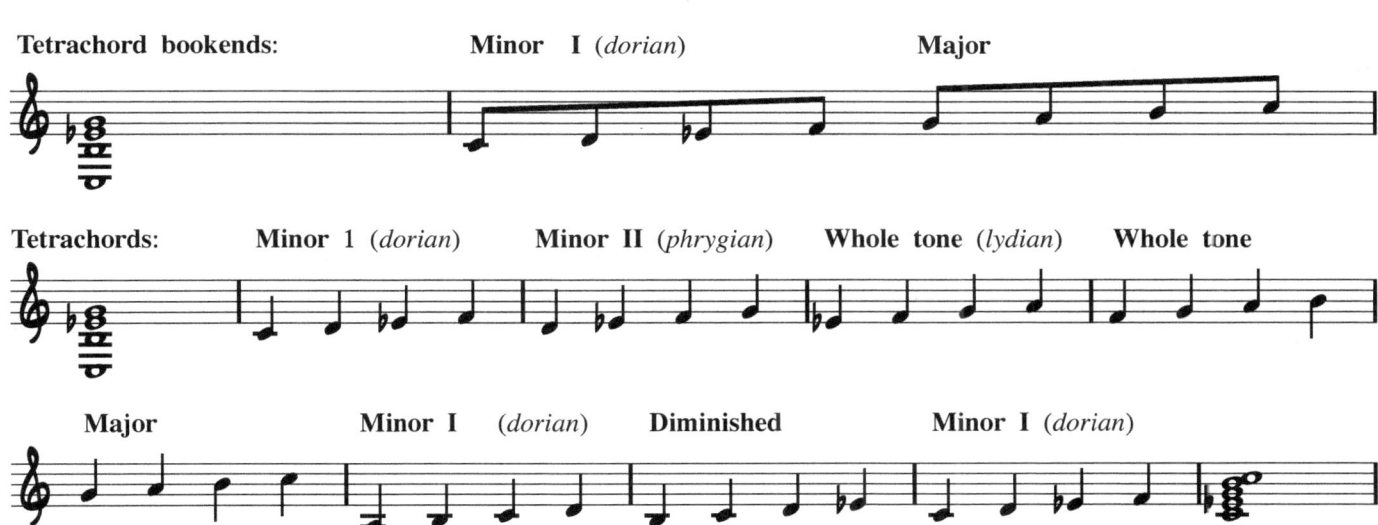

2nd Degree of C Melodic Minor

Chord Quality: Sus 7 (b9,13)

Chord: Dsus^(13b9)

Parallel: Phrygian Natural 6 (voice chord as EbMaj7#11/D)

Derivative: Play Melodic Minor starting from the 7th of chord

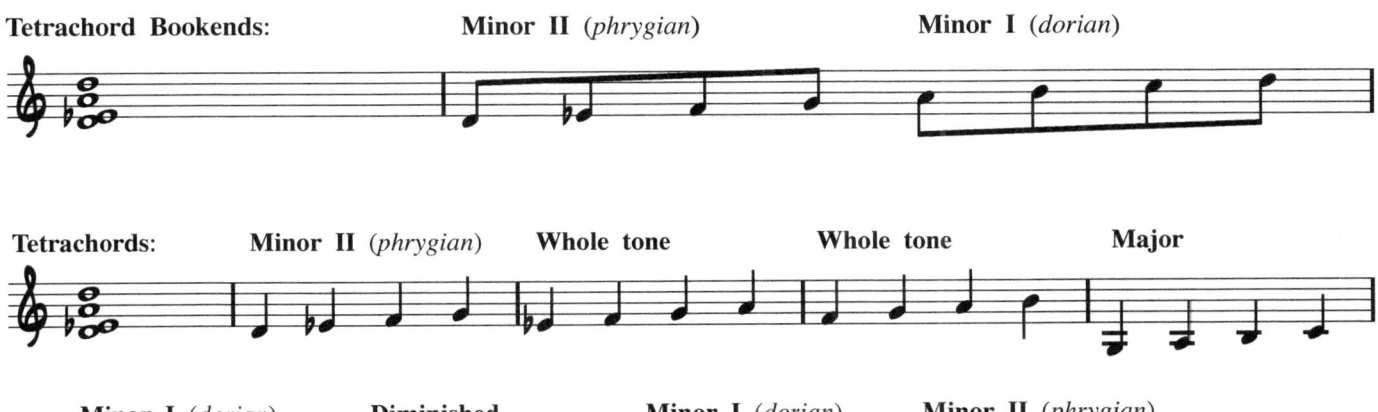

© Chris McNulty 2017

3rd Degree of C Melodic Minor

Chord Quality: (#11, +5, Maj 7, 9)

Chord: Eb+maj7

Parallel: Lydian Augmented from Root

Derivative: Play Melodic Minor from the 6th of the chord

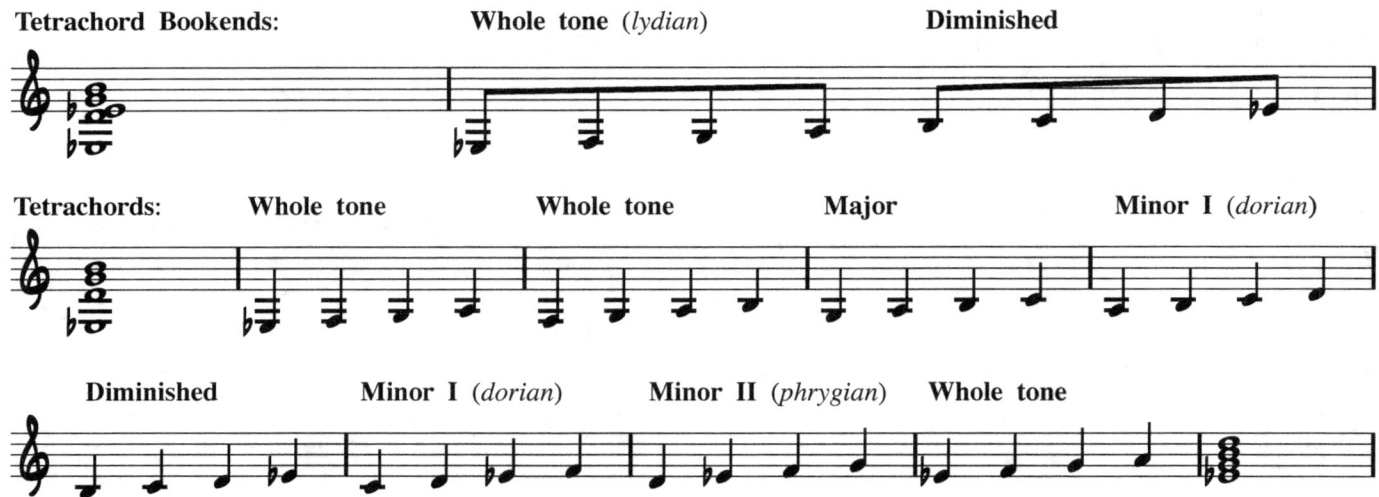

4th Degree of C Melodic

Chord Quality: (b7, 9, #11)

Chord: F7#11

Parallel: Lydian Dominant from Root

Derivative: Play C Melodic Minor from the 5th of the chord

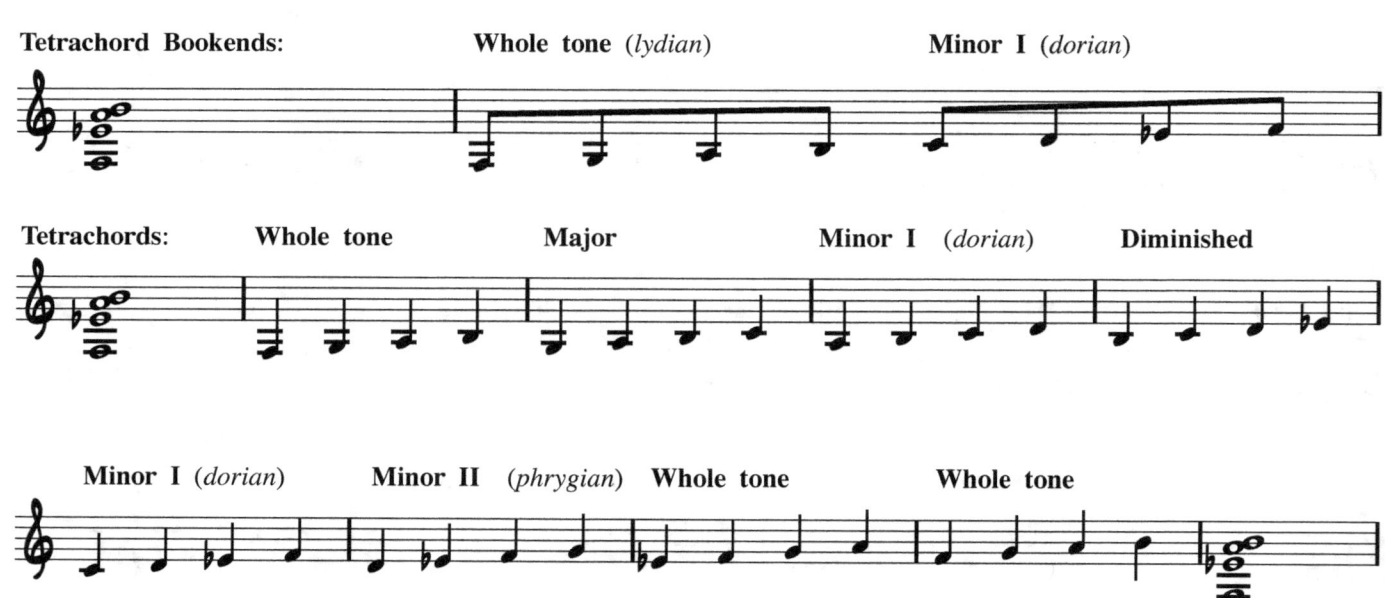

© Chris McNulty 2017

5th Degree of C Melodic Minor

Chord Quality: (b7, 11, b13)

Chord: G7b13

Parallel: Dom 7 b13 from Root

Derivative: Play Melodic Minor on the 4th of the chord

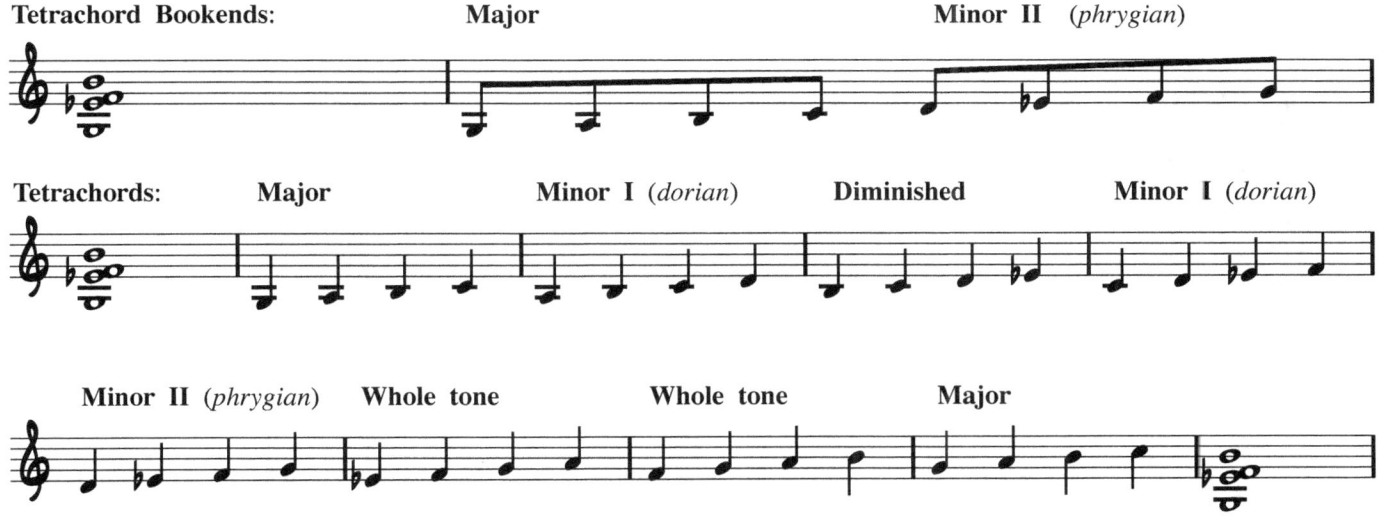

6th Degree of C Melodic Minor

Chord Quality: (nat2/9), b3, b5, b13, b7)

Chord: Ami b5

Parallel: Locrian - Nat 2 (1/2 Diminished) from Root

Derivative: Play Melodic Minor from the 3rd of the chord

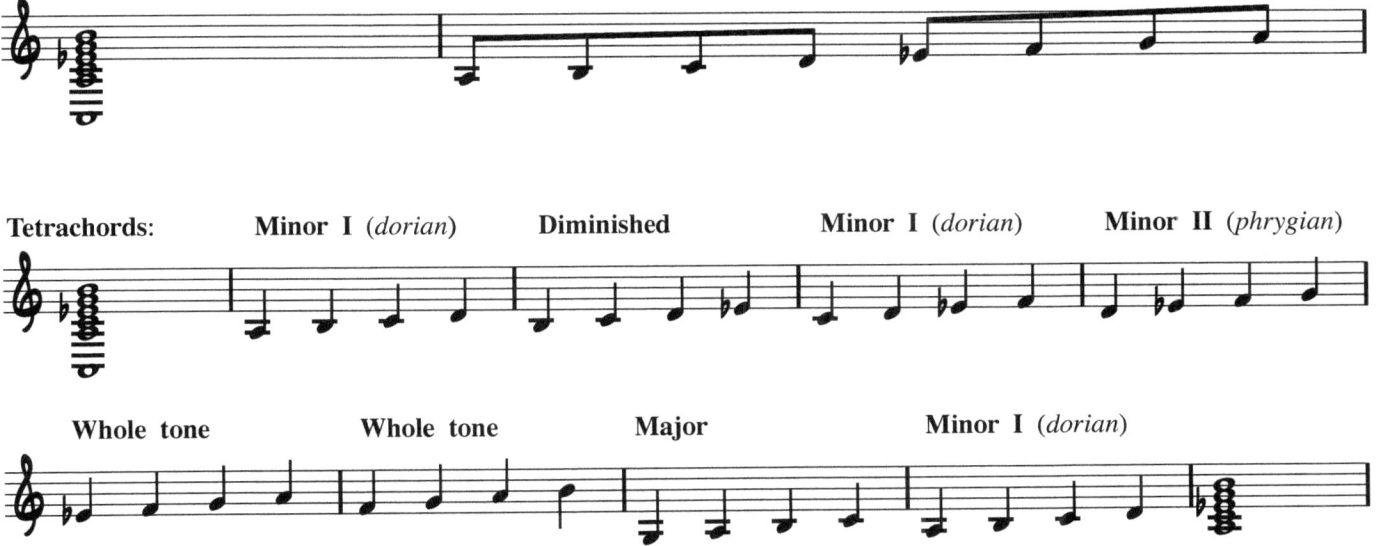

© Chris McNulty 2017

7th degree of Melodic Minor

Chord Type: Dom 7 (b9, #9, #11, no 5th, b13, b7)

Chord: B7b9#9#11b13

Parallel: Altered Scale from Root

Derivative: Play Melodic Minor from b9 of the chord

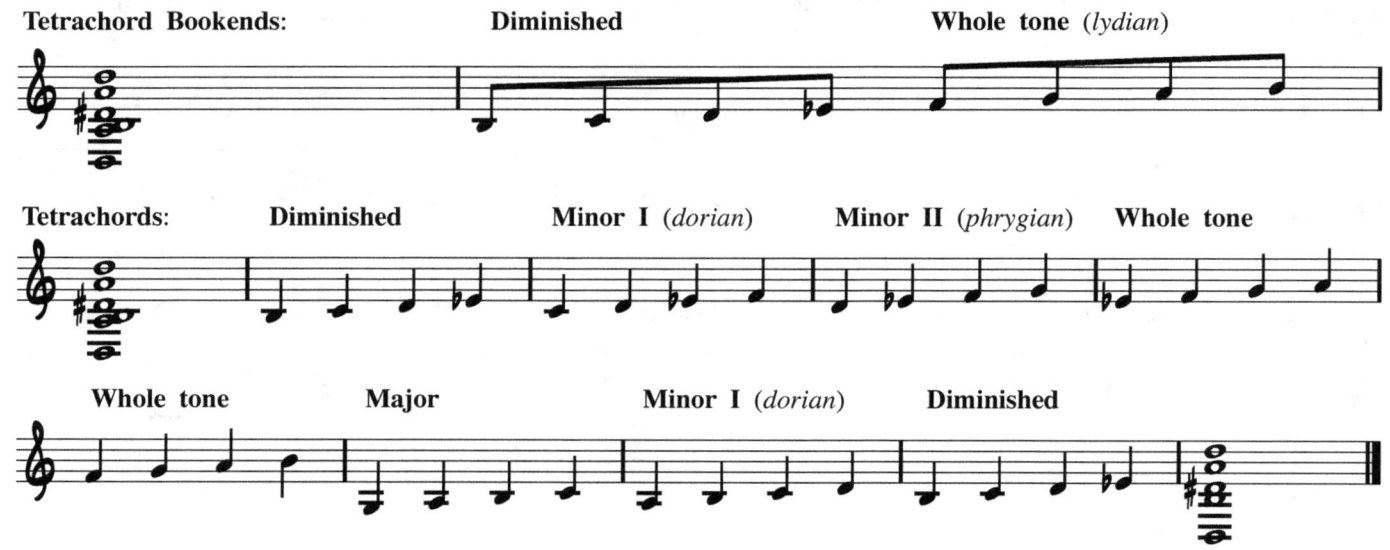

The Harmonic Minor Scale — (b3, b13, Maj 7)

The **Harmonic Minor** scale introduces us to the **Harmonic tetrachord** along with the all the tetrachords from the Melodic Minor and Major scales above. A Harmonic tetrachord includes a **minor 3rd** interval. The Harmonic Minor scale is where we first see the appearance of a "non-tetra chord" event. I've delineated with *** where they occur. Don't overly concern yourself with these "non-tetrachords" events. Our main interest is with three particular chord types that source from the 1st, 3rd and 5th degrees of the Harmonic Minor scale. The bookend tetrachords from each of these scales include one or more of the six tetrachords we're using in this methodology. One of my favorite scales comes from the **5th mode of the Harmonic Minor Scale - Arabic scale**.

Exercise 4 (track #4) — The Harmonic Minor Scale (b3, b13, Maj 7)

Introduces the **Harmonic** tetrachord (along with the five tetrachords from the Major and Melodic Minor scales).

The **1st mode** of "C" Harmonic Minor is C Harmonic Minor —
Chord CMin-Maj 7
Tetrachords: (1) **Minor I** (*dorian*) (C, D, Eb, F) and (2) **Harmonic** (G, Ab, B, C)

The **2nd mode: D 1/2 Diminished — Chord: D 1/2 Diminished**
Tetrachords: (1) **Minor II** (*phrygian*) (D, Eb, F, G) and (2) **Non-tetrachord event** (Ab, B, C, D)

The **3rd mode: E Augmented — Chord: Eb+maj7**
Tetrachords: (1) **Major** (Eb, F, G, Ab) and (2) **Diminished** (B, C, D, Eb)

The **4th mode: F Minor (#11) — Chord: F min 7 #11**
Tetrachords: (1) **Non-tetrachord event** (F, G, Ab, B) and (2) **Minor I** (C, D, Eb, F)

The **5th mode: G Arabic — Chord: G7 b9 b13**
Tetrachords: (1) **Harmonic** (G, Ab, B, C) and (2) **Minor II** (*phrygian*) (D, Eb, F, G)

© Chris McNulty 2017

The **6th mode: Ab Major (#9, #11)** — **Chord: AbMaj 7 #9, #11**
Tetrachords: (1) **Non-tetrachord event** (Ab, B, C, D) and (2) **Major** (Eb, F, G, Ab)

The **7th mode: B Diminished** — **Chord: B07**
Tetrachords: (1) **Diminished** (B, C, D, Eb) and (2) Non-tetrachord event (F, G, Ab, B)

4. Harmonic Minor
Scale-Chord use
using the C Harmonic Minor

*Track #4

1st Degree of C Harmonic Minor

Chord Quality: (1, 9, b3, 11, 5. b13, Maj 7)

Chord: Cm(maj7)

Parallel: C Harmonic Minor from Root of chord

Derivative: (same as above)

1st mode of scale is the only instance where parallel and derivative are one and the same

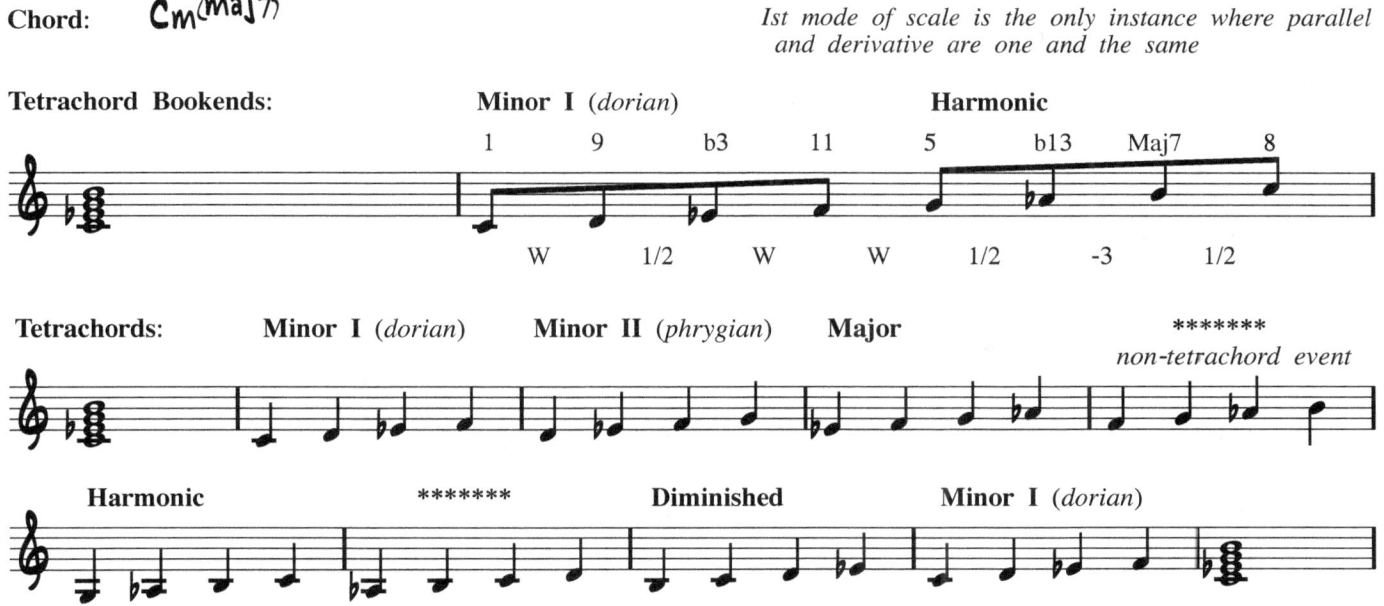

2nd Degree of Harmonic Minor

Chord Quality (1, b9, b3, 11, b5, nat 13, b7)

Chord: Dmi7b5b7

Parallel: Diminished 7, (b9, nat 13)

Derivative: Play Harmonic Minor from 7th of chord

© Chris McNulty 2017

3rd Degree of C Harmonic Minor

Chord Quality (1, 9, 3, 11, +5, nat 13, Maj 7)

Chord: Eb+maj7

Parallel: Play Augmented + Maj 7 (9, 11)

Derivative: Play Harmonic Minor from 6th of chord

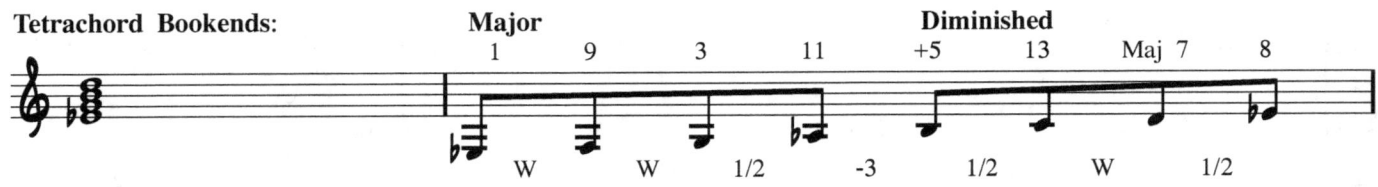

4th Degree of C Harmonic Minor

Chord Quality: (1, 9, b3, #11, 5, 13, b7)

Chord: Fmi7#11

Parallel: Play Minor 7, 9, #11, 13

Derivative: Play Harmonic Minor from 5th of chord

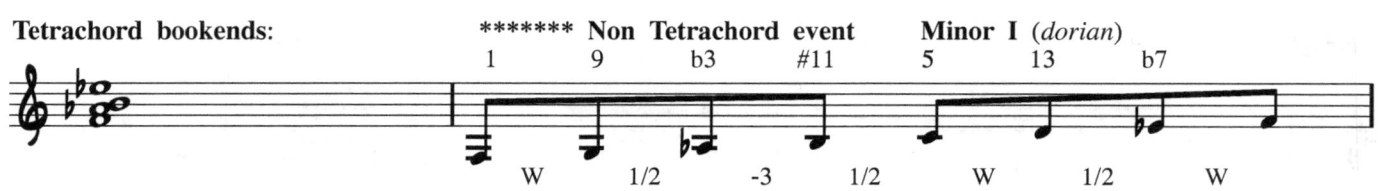

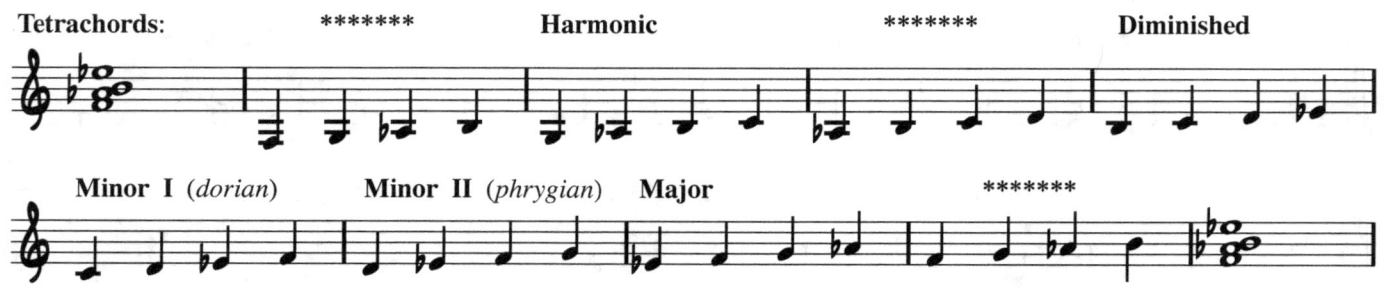

© Chris McNulty 2017

5th Degree of C Harmonic Minor
(also called the Arabic Scale)

Parallel: Play Arabic - Dom 7 (b9, b13)

Derivative: Play Harmonic Minor from 4th of chord

Chord Quality: (1, b9, 3, 11, 5, b13)

Chord: G7b9b13

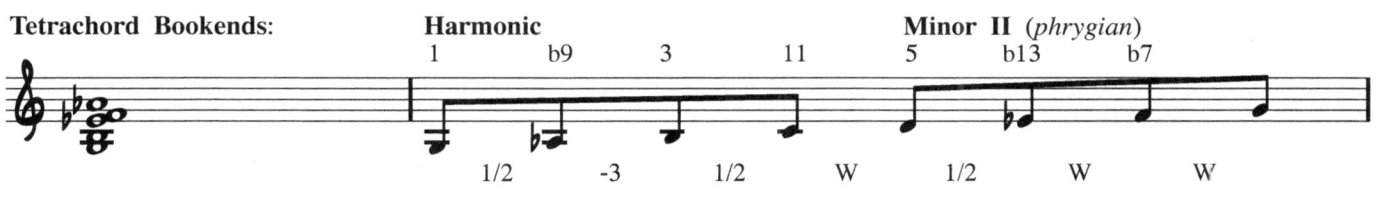

6th Degree of C Harmonic Minor

Parallel: Play Maj 7, #9, #11

Derivative: Play Harmonic Minor from the 3rd of the chord

Chord Quality: (1, #9, 3, #11, 5, 13, Maj 7)

Chord: Abma7#9#11

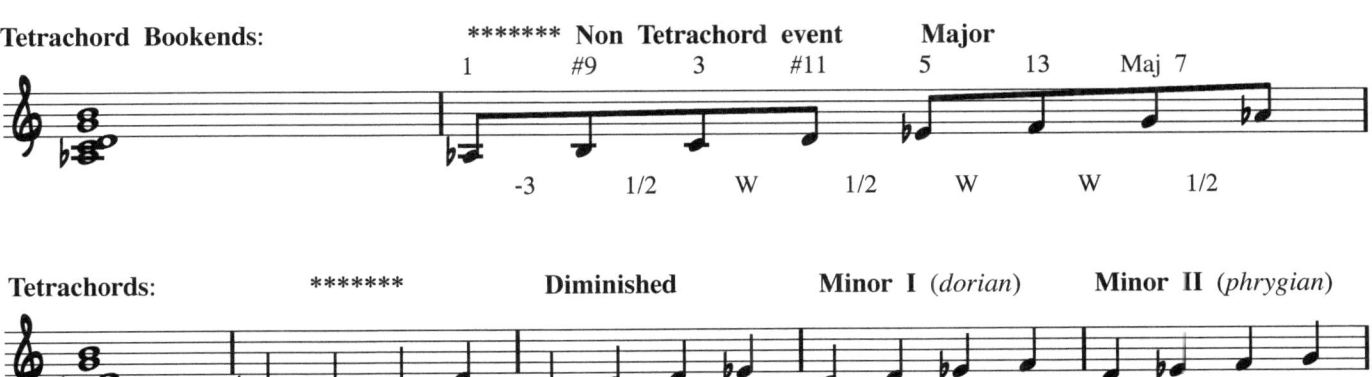

© Chris McNulty 2017

7th Degree of C Harmonic Minor   **Parallel:** Play Diminished (b9 #9, 3, #1, b13, bb7) from Root

Chord Quality (1, b9, #9, 3, #11, b13, bb7)   **Derivative:** Play Harmonic Minor from the b9 of the chord

Chord: B°7

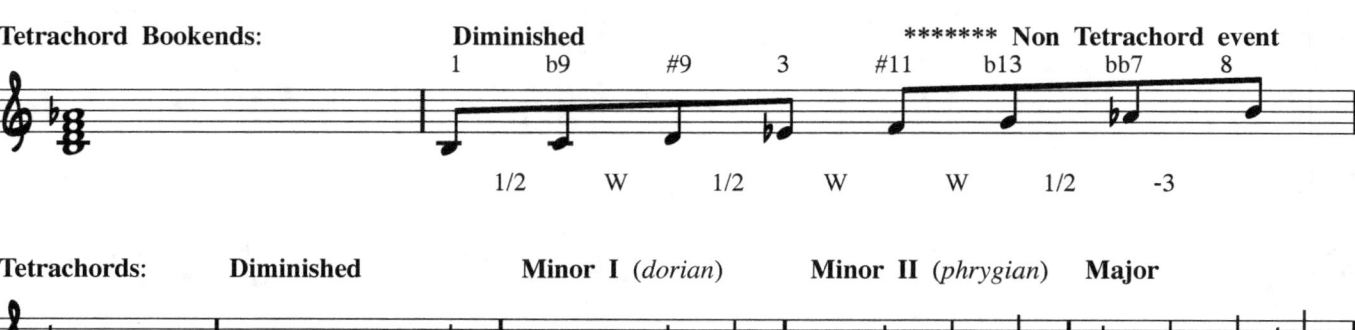

Exercise 5a (track #5) — The Altered Scale (7th mode of Melodic Minor) — Extra Drilling in all 12 keys.

Practice learning and hearing the **Altered Scale** over its accompanying Dom 7th chord quality **Augmented 7 (b9, #9, b13)**. This exercise will also reinforce the method behind learning how to identify, hear and utilize the difference between **Parallel** and **Derivative** use. I've included the exercises in all 12 keys to give you more time to integrate. By identifying the chord type and reading the notes, it not only becomes an extra theory drill but will improve your reading skills across all 12 keys. Learn to read in both treble and bass clef. We've sung/played the first six chords and left the remaining six for you to play/sing.

5a. The Altered Scale

*Track #5

(also known as the Diminished Whole Tone scale)
7th degree of the Melodic Minor
Derivative and Parallel scale & chord use

Chord: B+7#9 or B7(ALT)

Parallel: Play Altered Scale from B   Derivative: Use C Melodic Minor scale
Starting from the b2 of B+7#9

Tetrachord Bookends: Diminished   Whole tone   Minor I   Major

1 b9 #9 3 #11 b13 b7 8

Chord: E+7#9 or E7(ALT)

Parallel: Play Altered Scale from E   Derivative: Use F Melodic Minor scale
Starting from the b2 of E+7#9

Tetrachord Bookends: Diminished   Whole tone   Minor I   Major

Chord: A+7#9 or A7(ALT)

Parallel: Play Altered Scale from A   Derivative: Use Bb Melodic Minor scale
Starting from the b2 of A+7#9

Tetrachord Bookends: Diminished   Whole tone   Minor I   Major

Chord: D+7#9 or D7(ALT)

Parallel: Play Altered Scale from D   Derivative: Use Eb Melodic Minor scale
Starting from the b2 of D+7#9

Tetrachord Bookends: Diminished   Whole tone   Minor I   Major

© Chris McNulty 2017

Chord: G+7#9 or G7(ALT)

Parallel: Play Altered Scale from G

Derivative: Use Ab Melodic Minor scale
Starting from the b2 of G+7#9

Tetrachord Bookends: Diminished   Whole tone   Minor I   Major

Chord: C+7#9 or C7(ALT)

Parallel: Play Altered Scale from C

Derivative: Use Db Melodic Minor scale
Starting from the b2 of C+7#9

Tetrachord Bookends: Diminished   Whole tone   Minor I   Major

Chord: F+7#9 or F7(ALT)

Parallel: Play Altered Scale from F

Derivative: Use Gb Melodic Minor scale
Starting from the b2 of F+7#9

Tetrachord Bookends: Diminished   Whole tone   Minor I   Major

Chord: Bb+7#9 or Bb7(ALT)

Parallel: Play Altered Scale from Bb

Derivative: Use B Melodic Minor scale
Starting from the b2 of Bb+7#9

Tetrachord Bookends: Diminished   Whole tone   Minor I   Major

Chord: Eb+7#9 or Eb7(ALT)

Parallel: Play Altered Scale from Eb

Derivative: Use E Melodic Minor scale
Starting from the b2 of Eb+7#9

Tetrachord Bookends: Diminished   Whole tone   Minor I   Major

© Chris McNulty 2017

Chord: Ab+7#9 or Ab7(ALT)

Parallel: Play Altered Scale from Ab

Derivative: Use A Melodic Minor scale
Starting from the b2 of Ab+7#9

Tetrachord Bookends: Diminished   Whole tone   Minor I   Major

Chord: C#+7#9 or C#7(ALT)

Parallel: Play Altered Scale from C#

Derivative: Use D Melodic Minor scale
Starting from the b2 of C#+7#9

Tetrachord Bookends: Diminished   Whole tone   Minor I   Major

Chord: F#+7#9 or F#7(ALT)

Parallel: Play Altered Scale from F#

Derivative: Use G Melodic Minor scale
Starting from the b2 of F#+7#9

Tetrachord Bookends: Diminished   Whole tone   Minor I   Major

Outlining the tetrachords from each scale degree of the B Altered scale
(7th degree of C Melodic Minor Scale)

B+7(#9)   **Diminished**   **Minor I** (*dorian*)   **Minor II** (*phrygian*)   **Whole tone** (*lydian*)

Whole tone (*lydian*) **Major**   **Minor I** (*dorian*)   **Diminished**

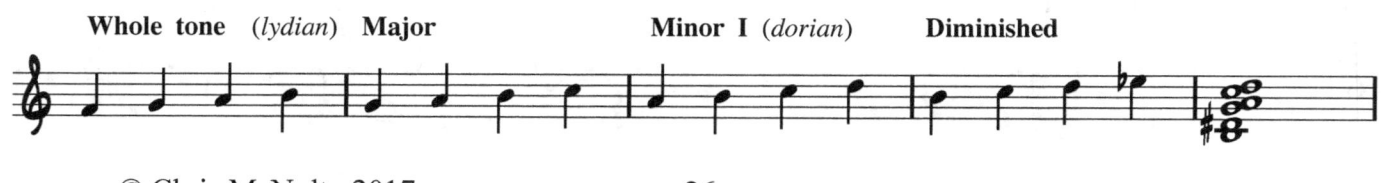

© Chris McNulty 2017

Exercise 5b (track #5) — Alternating between the Altered Scale and the Diminished (Half-whole)

The example in Ex. 5b demonstrates the subtler use of scales over a **Dominant 7 (b9, #9, b13 or nat 13)** chord. Both have the qualities of **b9, #9 & #11** in the first four notes which means the first tetrachord used is also the same (**Diminished**). The qualities of each chord differ from the 5th up (though they both include a b7) which means the scales differ, consequently making the 2nd tetrachord for each scale different (hence why we use two different scales) as follows:

We use the **Altered scale** when the 13th is flatted: **A7 (b9, #9, #11, b13)** ***NO 5th. If you've drilled sufficiently on Ex.5a you'll be familiar with the 2nd tetrachord in the **Altered scale** which is **Whole tone** (*lydian*).

We use the **Diminished scale** when the 13th is natural: **A7 (b9, #9, #11, Nat 13)**. The 2nd tetrachord is **Diminished** [*see Ex. 6a*]

I've used the same voicing for both chords: (LH) Root, 7th (RH, octave apart) 3rd, 7th, #9 Go to the piano and play this voicing using the sustain pedal and then alternate between singing or playing both scales.

5b. Alternating between the Altered Scale and Diminished Scale (half-whole)
Dom 7 Chords

* Track #5

Chord: A7(b9)   (b9, #9, Maj 3rd, #11, No 5th, b13)

Scale: Altered Scale   (7th mode of Bb Melodic Minor)

Tetrachords: Diminished   Whole tone (*lydian*)

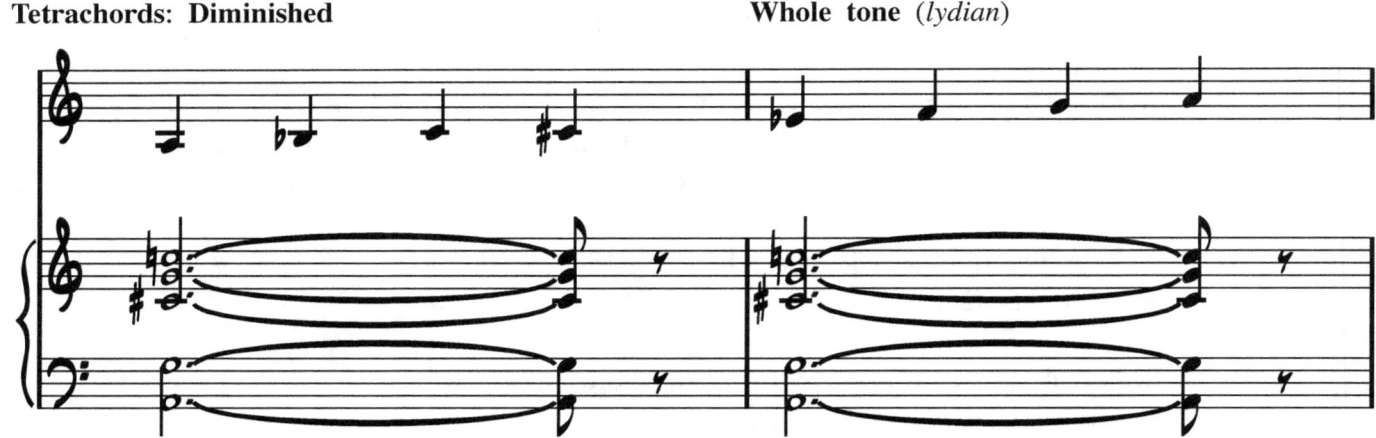

Chord: A7(b9)   (b9, #9, Maj 3, #11, 5th, Nat 13, b7)   *** 8 note scale

Scale: Diminished (Half-whole) scale

Tetrachords: Diminished   Diminished

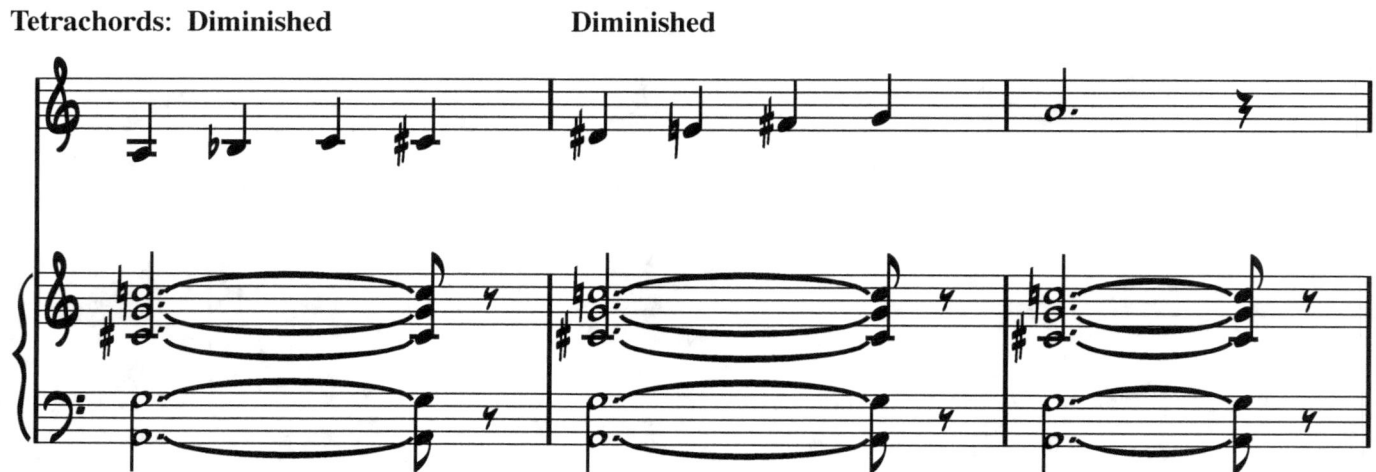

© Chris McNulty 2017

Exercise 5c (track #6) — The Arabic Scale (5th mode of Harmonic Minor) — Extra drilling over all 12 keys.

Practice learning/hearing the **Arabic Scale** over its accompanying **Dom 7th chord quality (b9, b13)**. These tools are provided to assist in identifying, hearing and utilizing the difference between **Parallel** and **Derivative** use.

5c. The Arabic Scale
5th Degree of Harmonic Minor

*Track #6

Remember the principal

Find the parent scale from looking at the degree

What is **G the 5th** of? = "C" [refer to Appendix 2]

Chord: G7b9b13

Derivative: Play C Harmonic minor
Starting from "C" (4th in G7b9)

Parallel: Play Arabic scale from the root "G"

Tetrachords: **Harmonic**   **Minor II** (*phrygian*)   **Minor I** (*dorian*) **Harmonic**

1 b9 3 11 5 b13 b7 8

1/2 -3 1/2 W 1/2 W W

Chord: C7b9b13

Derivative: Play F Harmonic minor
Starting from "F" (4th in C7b9)

Parallel: Play Arabic scale from the root "C"

Tetrachords: **Harmonic**   **Minor II** (*phrygian*)   **Minor I** (*dorian*) **Harmonic**

Chord: F7b9b13

Derivative: Play Bb Harmonic minor
Starting from Bb

Parallel: Play Arabic scale from "F"

Tetrachords: **Harmonic**   **Minor II** (*phrygian*)   **Minor I** (*dorian*) **Harmonic**

Chord: Bb7b9b13

Derivative: Play Eb Harmonic minor
Starting from Eb

Parallel: Play Arabic scale from "Bb"

Tetrachords: **Harmonic**   **Minor II** (*phrygian*)   **Minor I** (*dorian*) **Harmonic**

© Chris McNulty 2017

Chord: Eb7b9b13   **Derivative:** Play Ab Harmonic minor
Starting from Ab

Parallel: Play Arabic scale "Eb"

Tetrachords: Harmonic   Minor II (*phrygian*)   Minor I (*dorian*)   Harmonic

Chord: Ab7b9b13   **Derivative:** Play Db Harmonic minor
Starting from Db

Parallel: Play Arabic scale "Ab"

Tetrachords: Harmonic   Minor II (*phrygian*)   Minor I (*dorian*)   Harmonic

Chord: Db7b9b13   **Derivative:** Play Gb Harmonic minor
Starting from Gb

Parallel: Play Arabic scale "Db"

Tetrachords: Harmonic   Minor II (*phrygian*)   Minor I (*dorian*)   Harmonic

Chord: Gb7b9b13   **Derivative:** Play B Harmonic minor
Starting from B

Parallel: Play Arabic scale "Gb"

Tetrachords: Harmonic   Minor II (*phrygian*)   Minor I (*dorian*)   Harmonic

Chord: B7b9b13   **Derivative:** Play E Harmonic minor
Starting from E

Parallel Play Arabic scale from root "B"

Tetrachords: Harmonic   Minor II (*phrygian*)   Minor I (*dorian*)   Harmonic

© Chris McNulty 2017

Chord: **E7♭9♭13** Derivative: **Play A Harmonic minor**
Starting from A

Parallel: **Play Arabic scale "E"**

Tetrachords: **Harmonic**   **Minor II** (*phrygian*)   **Minor I** (*dorian*) **Harmonic**

Chord: **A7♭9♭13** Derivative: **Play D Harmonic minor**
Starting from D

Parallel: **Play Arabic scale "A"**

Tetrachords: **Harmonic**   **Minor II** (*phrygian*)   **Minor I** (*dorian*) **Harmonic**

Chord: **D7♭9♭13** Derivative: **Play G Harmonic minor**
Starting from G

Parallel: **Play Arabic scale "D"**

Tetrachords: **Harmonic**   **Minor II** (*phrygian*)   **Minor I** (*dorian*) **Harmonic**

Outlining the tetrachords of each degree of the G Arabic scale (5th degree of C Harmonic Minor Scale)

G7♭9♭13

Tetrachords: **Harmonic**   ***********   **Diminished**   **Minor I** (*dorian*)
non tetrachord event

Minor II (*phyrgian*) **Major**   ***********   **Harmonic**

© Chris McNulty 2017

Chapter Four — The Diminished Scales

There are two types of **Diminished** scales (1) **Half-whole** and (2) **Whole-half**.

- The **Half-whole** sequence is used over **Dom** 7 chords (**b9, #9, #11, 13**)
- The **Whole-half** sequence is used over **Diminished** 7 chords (9, b3, b5, b13, bb7, maj7)

Let's start with the **Diminished (Half-whole) Scale** sequence first.

Exercise 6a (track #7) — The Diminished (Half-whole) Scale

There are only **three Diminished (Half-whole) Scales** — C, Db and D
 Each of these scales work over four **Dom** 7 (**b9, #9, 13**) chords
 Play each scale in **Half-whole step motion** from the **root** of the chord.
 All chord and tension tones are a Minor 3rd apart.

C Diminished (Half-whole) scale — (**C**, **Db**, **Eb**, E, **Gb**, G, **A**, Bb, **C**) works over the following four chords:

C7 (b9, #9 13)   **Eb7** (b9, #9 13)   **Gb7** (b9, #9 13)   **A7** (b9, #9 13)

  Starting from "C"   play **C7** (b9, #9 13)
  Starting from "Eb" play **Eb7** (b9, #9 13)
  Starting from "Gb" play **Gb7** (b9, #9 13)
  Starting from "A"   play **A7** (b9, #9 13)

Db Diminished (Half-whole) scale — (**Db**, D, **E**, F **G**, Ab, **Bb**, B, **Db**) works over the following four chords:

Db7 (b9, #9 13)   **E7** (b9, #9 13)   **G7** (b9, #9 13)   **Bb7** (b9, #9 13)

  Starting from "Db" play **Db7** (b9, #9 13)
  Starting from "E"   play **E7** (b9, #9 13)
  Starting from "G"   play **G7** (b9, #9 13)
  Starting from "Bb" play **Bb7** (b9, #9 13)

© Chris McNulty 2017

D Diminished (Half-whole) scale — (**D**, Eb, **F**, F#, **G#**, A, **B**, C **D**) works over the following four chords:

D7 (b9, #9 13)   **F7** (b9, #9 13)   **G#7** (b9, #9 13)   **B7** (b9, #9 13)

        Starting from "**D**" play **D7** (b9, #9 13)
        Starting from "**F**" play **F7** (b9, #9 13)
        Starting from "**G#**" play **G#7** (b9, #9 13)
        Starting from "**B**" play **B7** (b9, #9 13)

6a. Using the Diminished (Half-whole) scale over Dom 7 (b9, #9, 13) chords

*Track #7

Key to working with the **Diminished (Half-whole)** scale over **Dominant 7 b9 nat** chords

Always use **Half-whole** motion from root of chord: **1, b9, #9, 3, #11, 5, nat 13, b7**

There are only three Diminished scales: **C Diminished, Db Diminished and D Diminished**

Each scale works over 4 chords each (there are 12 chords in total)

Chord and tension tones are always a Minor 3rd apart

C Diminished Scale (Half-whole) works over the following **Dominant 7(b9,#9,13)** chords:

Chords:

Chords: C7(b9)   A7(b9)   Gb9   Eb7(b9)   C7(b9)
Tetrachords: Minor I   Minor I

The Tetrachords starting from each scale degree alternate between Diminished & Minor I

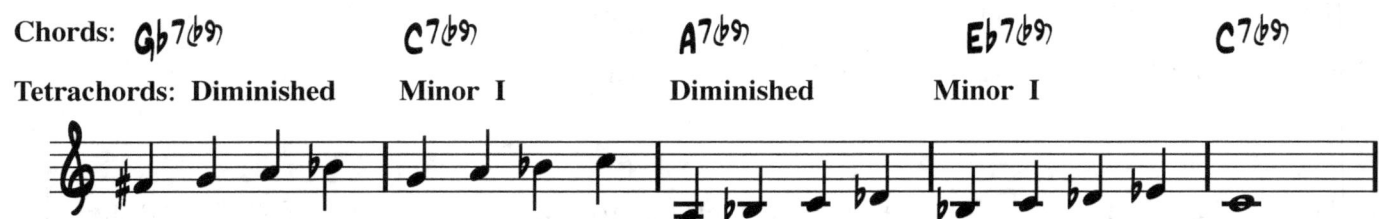

For extra drilling practice sing/play the Chords and Tension tones:

Chord tones: Root, 3rd, 5th, b7

At piano play chord in LH (using sustain pedal) and in RH sing/play the chord/tension tones

Practice singing Tension tones: b9, #11, 13, b9

Starting from the Root followed by tension tones

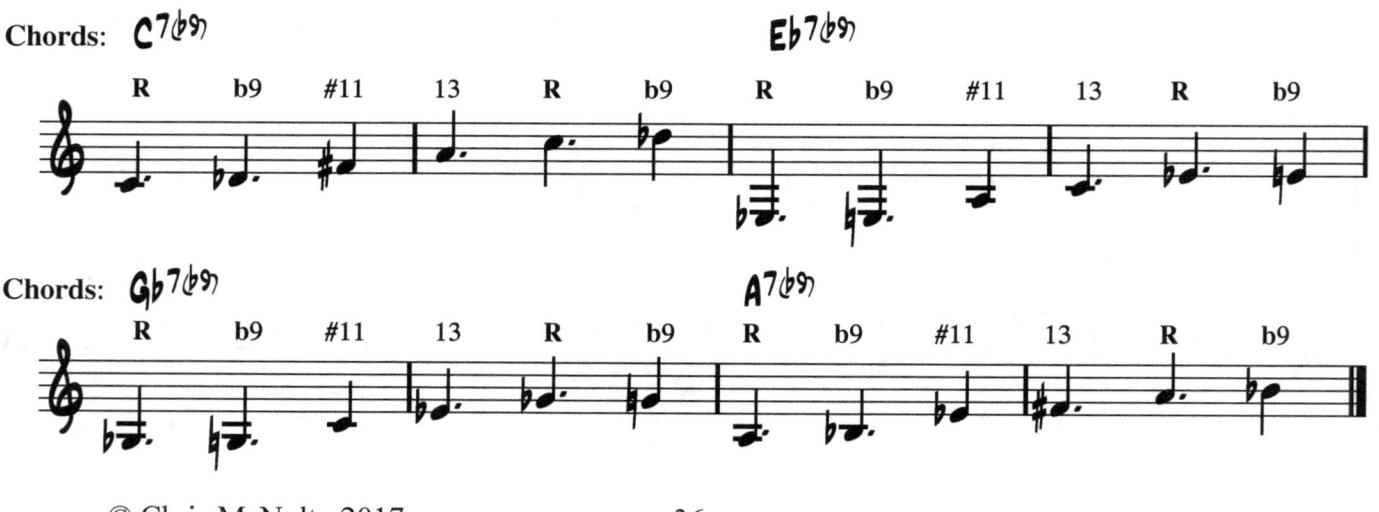

© Chris McNulty 2017

Db Diminished (Half-whole) scale works over the following four Dom 7 b9 chords:

Chords: Db7(b9)   E7(b9)   G7(b9)   Bb7(b9)

Chords: Db7(b9)   E7(b9)   G7(b9)   Bb7(b9)   Db7(b9)
Tetrachords: Diminished   Diminished

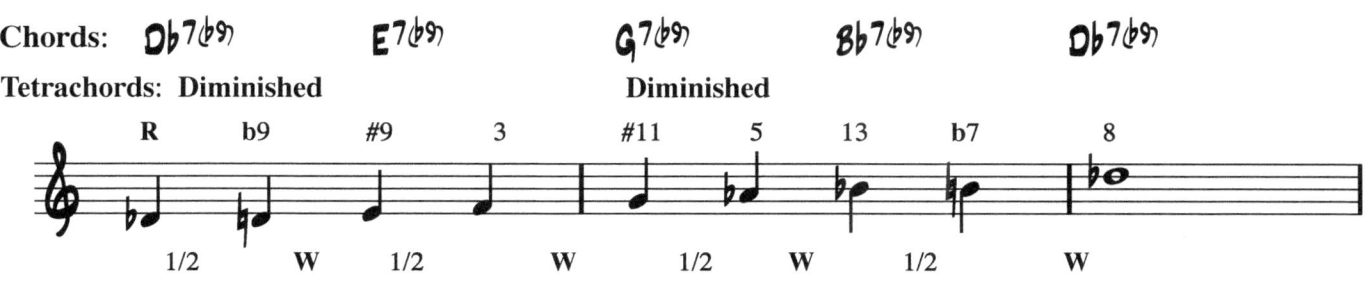

Chords: Db7(b9)   E7(b9)   G7(b9)   Bb7(b9)   Db7(b9)
Tetrachords: Minor I   Minor I

Tetrachords starting from each scale degree alternate between Diminished & Minor I (*dorian*)

Chords: Db7(b9)   G7(b9)   E7(b9)   Bb7(b9)
Tetrachords: Diminished   Minor I   Diminished   Minor I

Chords: G7(b9) Db7(b9) Bb7(b9) E7(b9) Db7(b9)

Tetrachords: Diminished Minor I Diminished Minor I

For extra drilling practice sing/play the Chords and Tension tones:

Chord tones: Root, 3rd, 5th, b7

At piano play chord in LH (using sustain pedal) and in RH sing/play the chord/tension tones

Chords: Db7(b9) E7(b9) G7(b9) Bb7(b9)

Practice singing Tension tones: b9, #11, 13, octave, b9

Starting from root followed by tension tones

Chords: Db7(b9) E7(b9)

Chords: G7(b9) Bb7(b9)

D Diminished (Half-whole) scale works over the following Dom 7 (b9, #9, 13) chords:

For extra drilling practice sing/play the Chords and Tension tones:

Chord tones: Root, 3rd, 5th, b7

At piano play chord in LH (using sustain pedal) and in RH sing/play the chord/tension tones

Practice singing/playing Tension tones: b9, #11, 13, Octave, b9

Starting from the root followed by tension tones

© Chris McNulty 2017

Exercise 7 (track #8) — The Diminished (Whole-half) Scale

This scale is used over Diminished 7 chords

> There are only **three Diminished scales (Whole-half)**: C, Db and D
> Use **Whole-half motion** from **Root**: 1, 9, b3, 11, b5, b13, bb7, Maj7.
> We use the notation ° to delineate "Diminished" chords
> All chord and tension tones are a **Minor 3rd** apart.

Each scale works over **four Diminished 7 chords** each as follows:

> **C Diminished** scale is used over: **C°, Eb°, Gb°, A°**
> **Db Diminished** scale is used over: **Db°, E°, G°, Bb°**
> **D Diminished** scale is used over: **D°, F°, Ab°, B°**

The exercise below shows you the four chords that work with each of the three scales.

7a. Using the Diminished (Whole-Half) Scale over Diminished 7 chords

*Track #8

Use **Whole-half step** motion from Root: 1, 9, b3, 11, b5, b13, bb7, Maj7

There are only three Diminished scales: **C, Db and D**

Each of these three scales works with 4 specific Diminished chords

Chord and tension tones are all a Minor 3rd apart

C Diminished scale works over the following 4 Diminished chords: C°7 Eb°7 Gb°7 A°7

Tetrachords from each scale degree alternate between Minor I (*dorian*) **& Diminished**

Chords:	C°7	Eb°7	Gb°7	A°7
Tetrachords:	Minor I	Diminished	Minor I	Diminished

© Chris McNulty 2017

Chords: E♭°7   G♭°7   A°7   C°7
Tetrachords: Minor I   Diminished   Minor I   Diminished

For extra drilling practice - Sing and play   Chord ands Tension tones

Chord tones: Root, b3rd, b5th, 6th (bb7)

Use sustain pedal to play chord in LH and in RH play/sing chord/tension tones RH

Chords: C°7   E♭°7   G♭°7   A°7
R b3 b5 bb7   R b3 b5 bb7   R b3 b5 bb7   R b3 b5 bb7   8

Sing/play Tension tones - 9th, 11th, b13, Maj 7   * ALL intervals are a minor 3rd apart**

*** *Especially when dealing with tension tones always play the chord first and pitch from the root note)*

Chords: C°7   E♭°7
R 9 11 b13 maj7 R   R 9 11 b13 maj7 R

Chords: G♭°7   A°7   C°7
R 9 11 b13 maj7 R   R 9 11 b13 maj7 R

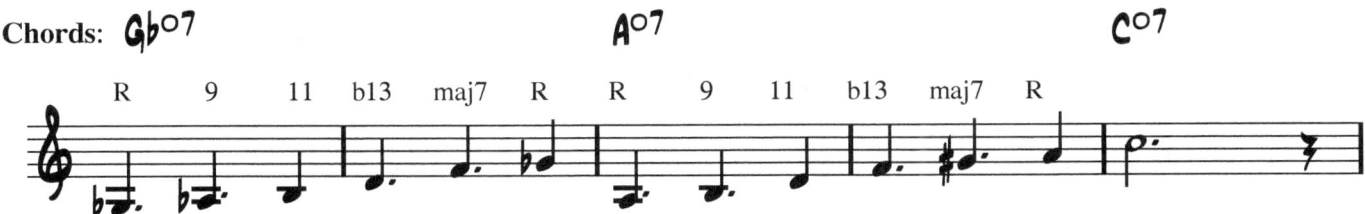

Db Diminished Scale works over the following 4 Diminished chords: D♭°7 E°7 G°7 B♭°7

D♭°7   E°7   G°7   B♭°7

© Chris McNulty 2017

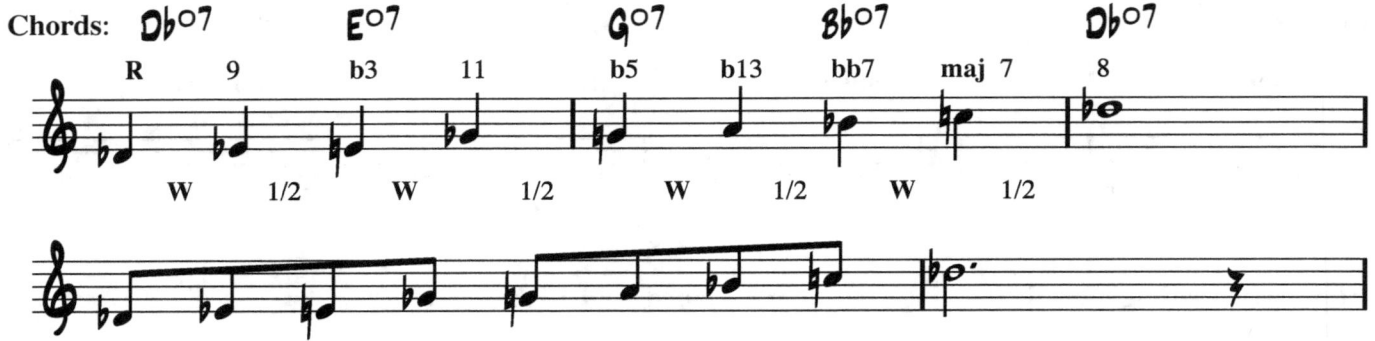

Tetrachords from each scale degree alternate between Minor I (*dorian*) **& Diminished**

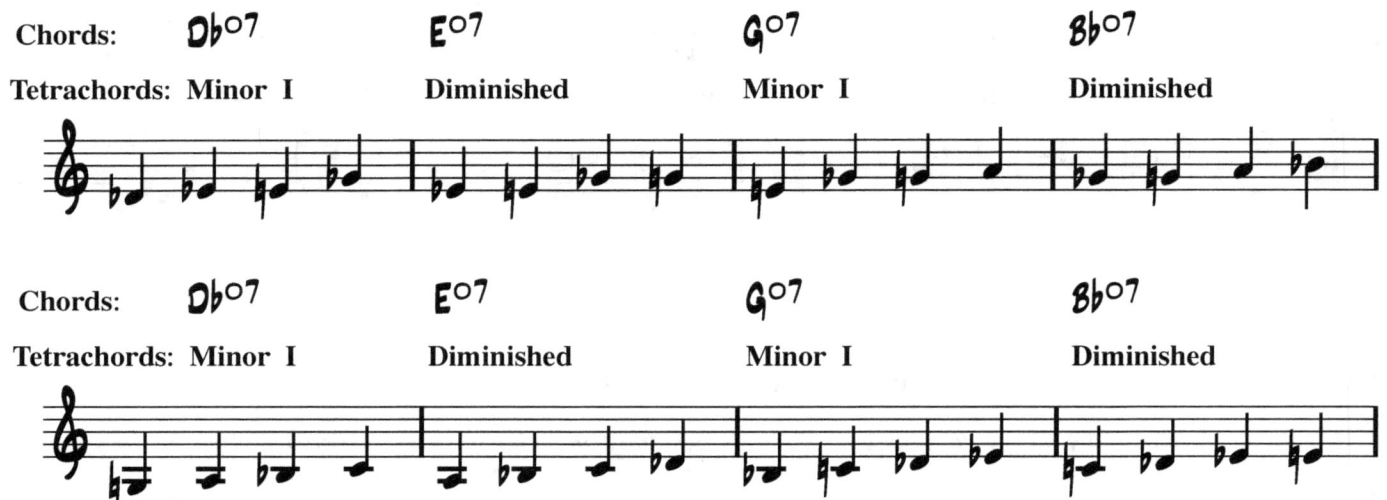

As an extra drilling exercise sing/play Chord and Tension tones

Chort tones: Root, b3rd, b5th, 6th (bb7)

Use sustain pedal to play chord in LH and in RH sing/play chord/tension tones

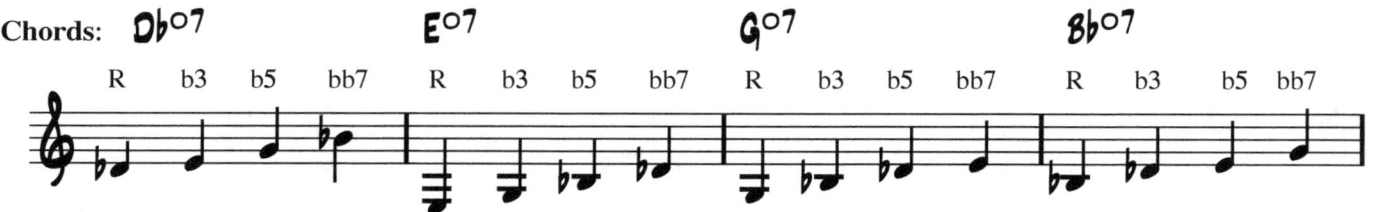

Tension tones: 9th, 11th, b13, Maj 7

***Especially when dealing with tension tones always play the chord first and pitch from the root note

D Diminished Scale works over the following 4 Diminished chords: D°7 F°7 Ab°7 B°7

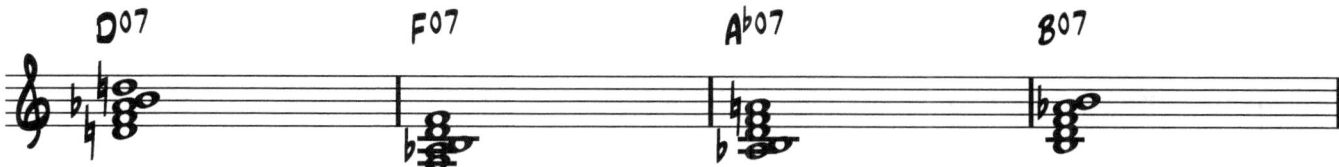

As an extra drilling exercise sing/play Chord and Tension tones

Chord tones: Root, b3rd, b5th, 6th (bb7)

Sing/play Tension tones - 9th, 11th, b13, Maj 7

**** Especially when dealing with tension tones always play the chord first and pitch from the root note

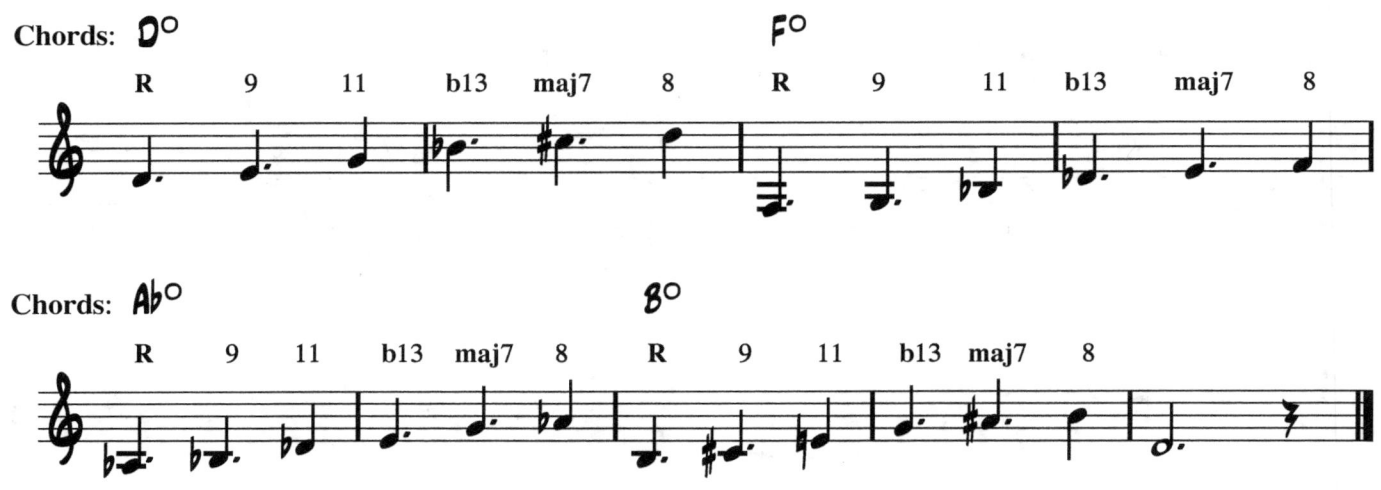

Chapter Five — Singing tetrachords over harmony using one root for each key

Exercise 8 — (tracks #9 & #10 with Trio)

I've chosen a random set of chord changes to sing this first exercise. It's a very simple way to start the process of integrating the **six tetrachords** over simple harmony while giving you the tools for building your own exercises. The chord progression stays the same throughout all twelve (12) keys as does the system of starting each tetrachord on the same note for each key event. The order of how they appear is also the same. For instance, starting in the **Key of "F,"** each of the six tetrachords occur in exactly the same order throughout the entire exercise as does the chord quality type. Similarly each tetrachord uses the same root note to build from for each "key."

For example:

- "F" is the tonic on the first chord **Fmaj7#11**
- "F" becomes the 13th on the following chord **Abmaj7,**
- "F" the 9th for the next **Ebmin7**
- "F" the 5th for **Bbmaj/min7**
- "F" the 7th on **Gmin7**
- "F" the major 7th of the diminished chord **F#dim** so on and so forth for the proceeding keys.

At each "chord event," the tetrachord is sung up and down resolving to a specific note in the chord before moving to the next chord event. For example the opening chord of **Fmaj7 #11** resolves to its major 7th **"E"** before pitching to the next tetrachord which once again starts on "F." The next chord **AbMaj7** resolves to its major 3rd and so on and so forth. After singing ALL six tetrachords over the chord progression in **"F"** we then move up a half-step up to the key of **F#** using exactly the same chord progression and system of tetrachords in the new key. This time starting on F# and so on and so forth.

This exercise has no other singular importance than to integrate the sound of each tetrachord over different chord qualities/types and example how singing up and down each tetrachord over a chord quality works melodically over a chord. It's NOT scale work. Exercise 9 **"Singing over II, V, I, VI harmony"** addresses those principles.

You can switch octaves whenever you need to. I've provided you with two tracks to sing over. Track 9 is a medium bossa nova feel (using a 3-2 clave). My voice is there as a guide on Track 9 however I've left track 10 voiceless so you can sing along without my voice as a guide. Practice with me first and then move on to track 10. *** For homework find your own set of changes and use these six tetrachords in any order that suits but continue using the system of choosing same root note for each key system. You'll be surprised how many options you have. To make it work you'll have to come up with a set of chord qualities that sound good played consecutively.

8. Singing Tetrachords over Harmony
using same root note (each key)

Sing Whole tone (*lydian*) **tetrachord up and down resolve to major 7th**

Sing Minor I (*dorian*) **tetrachord up and down resolve to major 3rd**

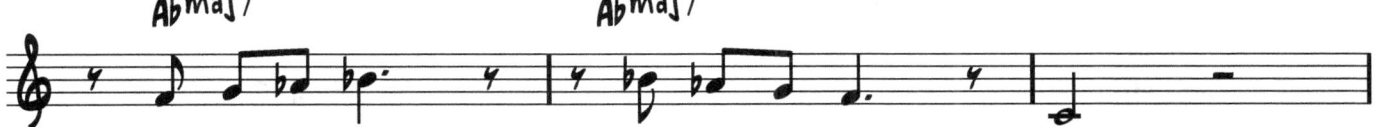

Sing Minor II (*phrygian*) **tetrachord up and down resolve to minor 7th**

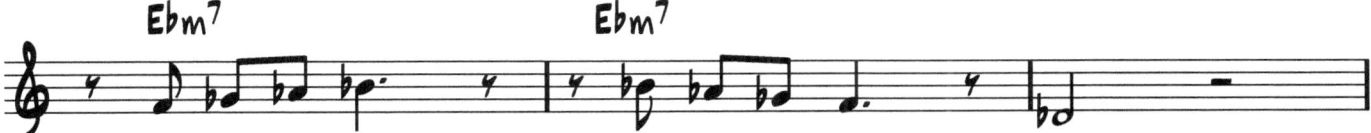

Sing Harmonic tetrachord up and down resolve to major 7th

Sing Major tetrachord up and down resolve to 5th

Sing Diminished tetrachord up and down resolve to bb7

Sing Whole tone (*lydian*) **tetrachord up and down resolve to major 7th**

Sing Minor I (*dorian*) **tetrachord up and down resolve to 3rd**

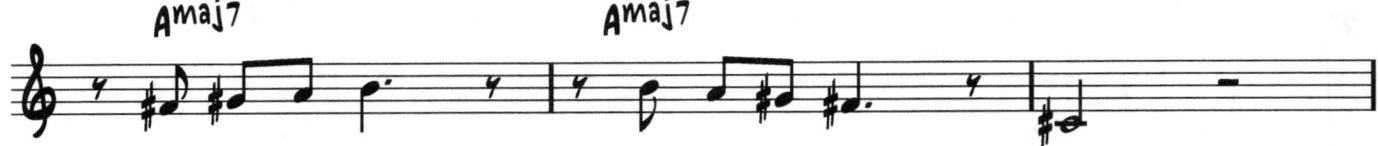

Sing Minor II (*phrygian*) **tetrachord up and down resolve to minor 7th**

Sing Harmonic tetrachord up and down resolve to major 7th

Sing Major tetrachord up and down resolve up to 5th

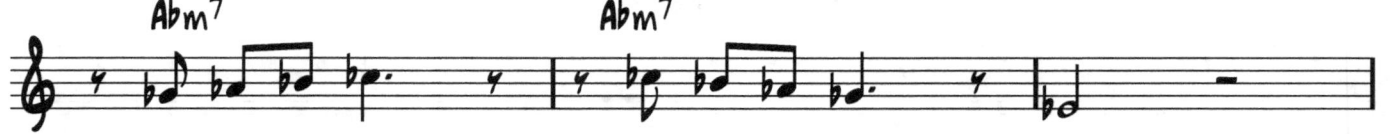

Sing Diminished tetrachord up and down resolve to bb7th

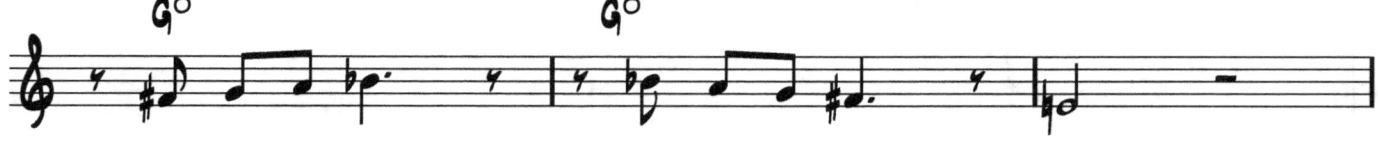

© Chris McNulty 2017

Sing Whole tone (*lydian*) **tetrachord up and down resolve to major 7th**

Sing Minor I (*dorian*) **tetrachord up and down resolve to 3rd**

Sing Minor II (*phrygian*) **tetrachord up and down resolve to minor 7th**

Sing Harmonic tetrachord up and down resolve to major 7th

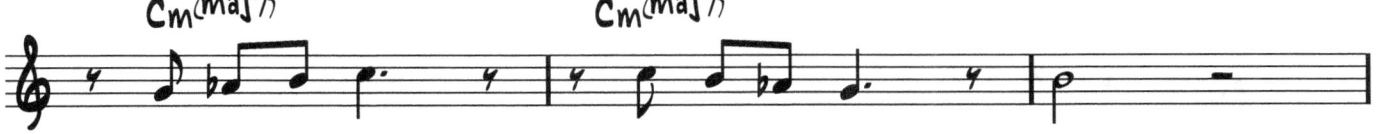

Sing Major tetrachord up and down resolve to 5th

Sing Diminished tetrachord up and down resolve to bb7

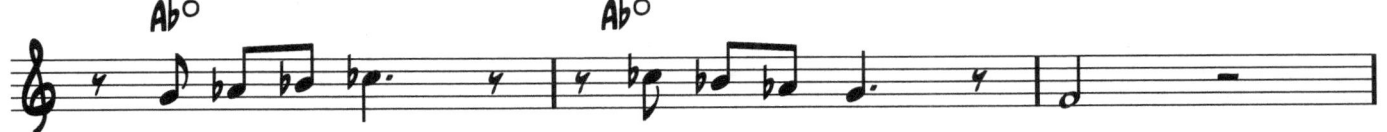

Sing Whole tone (*lydian*) **tetrachord up and down resolve to major 7th**

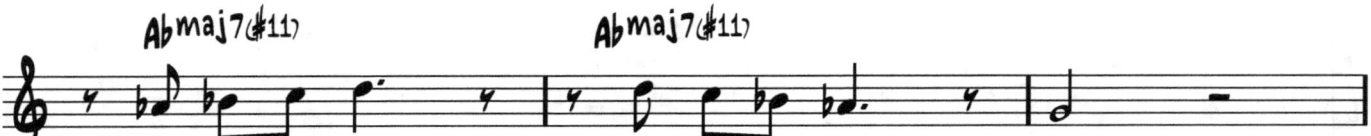

Sing Minor I (*dorian*) **tetrachord up and down resolve to major 3rd**

Sing Minor II (*phrygian*) **tetrachord up and down resolve to minor 7th**

Sing Harmonic tetrachord up and down resolve to major 7th

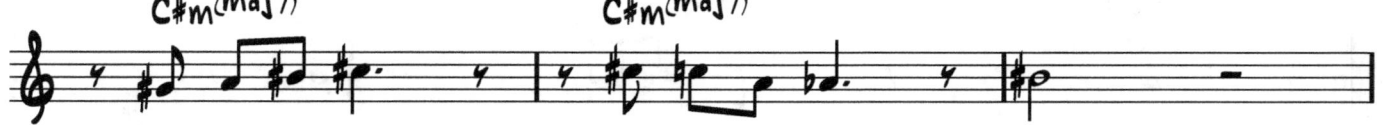

Sing Major tetrachord up and down resolve to 5th

Sing Diminished tetrachord up and down resolve to bb7

© Chris McNulty 2017

Sing Whole tone (*lydian*) **tetrachord up and down resolve to major 7th**

Sing Minor I (*dorian*) **tetrachord up and down resolve to major 3rd**

Sing Minor II (*phrygian*) **tetrachord up and down resolve to minor 7th**

Sing Harmonic tetrachord up and down resolve to major 7th

Sing Major tetrachord up and down resolve to 5th

Sing Diminished tetrachord up and down resolve to bb7

Sing Whole tone (*lydian*) **tetrachord up and down resolve to major 7th**

Sing Minor I (*dorian*) **tetrachord up and down resolve to major 3rd**

Sing Minor II (*phrygian*) **tetrachord up and down resolve to minor 7th**

Sing Harmonic tetrachord up and down resolve to major 7th

Sing Major tetrachord up and down resolve to 5th

Sing Diminished tetrachord up and down resolve to bb7

© Chris McNulty 2017

Sing Whole tone (*lydian*) **tetrachord up and down resolve to major 7th**

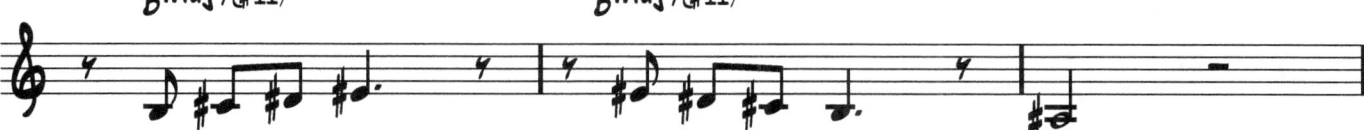

Sing Minor I (*dorian*) **tetrachord up and down resolve to major 3rd**

Sing Minor II (*phrygian*) **tetrachord up and down resolve to minor 7th**

Sing Harmonic tetrachord up and down resolve to major 7th

Sing Major tetrachord up and down resolve to 5th

Sing Diminished tetrachord up and down resolve to bb7

© Chris McNulty 2017

Sing Whole tone (*lydian*) **tetrachord up and down resolve to major 7th**

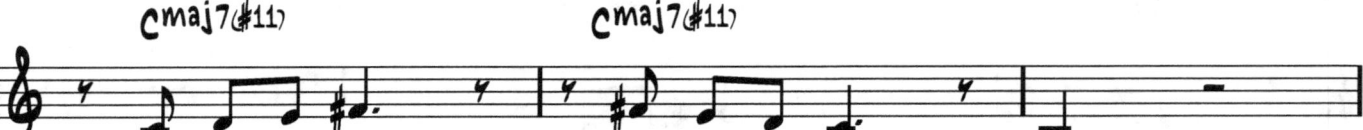

Sing Minor I (*dorian*) **tetrachord up and down resolve to major 3rd**

Sing Minor II (*phrygian*) **tetrachord up and down resolve to minor 7th**

Sing Harmonic tetrachord up and down resolve to major 7th

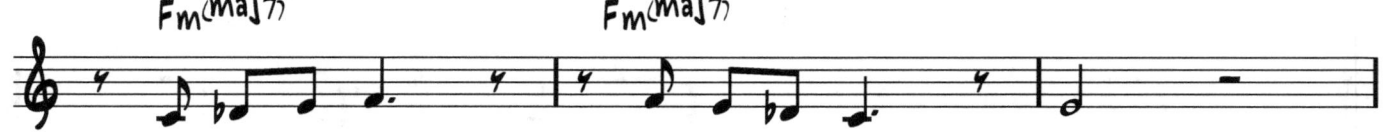

Sing Major tetrachord up and down resolve to 5th

Sing Diminished tetrachord up and down resolve to bb7

Sing Whole tone (*lydian*) **tetrachord up and down resolve to major 7th**

Sing Minor I (*dorian*) **tetrachord up and down resolve to major 3rd**

Sing Minor II (*phrygian*) **tetrachord up and down resolve to minor 7th**

Sing Harmonic tetrachord up and down resolve to major 7th

Sing Major tetrachord up and down resolve to 5th

Sing Diminished tetrachord up and down resolve to bb7

Chapter Six — Singing scales using tetrachords over II, V, I, VI progression.

Exercise 9a (track #11) - Preparation: Singing the tetrachords over the first progression (starting in the key of C)

This exercise gives you the opportunity to apply what you've learned in the prior chapters by taking it to the next step, singing over a **II, V, I, VI** pattern with passing chords leading you to the next key. I'm assuming that students already have a basic understanding of roman numeral sequence as it applies to chordal harmony. All the scales and associated chords which appear in this exercise should be somewhat familiar from the work we've done in the prior exercises. Before digging in, take a little time to familiarize yourself with the information included in the first two measures. It will help immeasurably. Practice singing/playing along with my voice before moving to Ex.9b. Outside of the key notation, four (4) important pieces of information are provided on the stave for each event as follows:

- **Chord** — the **Roman Numeric** sequence and the chord quality
- **Scale choice** — stating both **Parallel** or **Derivative** options
- **Tetrachords** — each **Tetrachord** that bookends or outlines the scale
- **Piano short cut** — The use of **slash/chords** as an easier way of voicing a chord

Each section or key mirrors the same information as the prior key. When the tetrachord starts from the **Root** of the chord, I'm using **Parallel** usage. When it begins on the **Parent scale**, starting on the b9, #11, 3rd or 5th I'm using **Derivative** (*for further explanation see Appendix 2 - Parallel & Derivative uses*). I've included both **Parallel** and **Derivative** choices to give you a chance to try different combinations of tetrachords (out of the six you've learned) BUT also to show you how different each of them sound.

I've switched octaves based on what I think will be most comfortable for the female voice. Please feel free to continue in an upward direction if you have the range or start an octave lower. Wherever I mention two scale options, I've tried to use both throughout the exercise.

Utilize the Appendices wherever indicated. These are not just useful resource tools but also work as excellent drilling exercises to help integrate the theory behind much of the work you're doing. I hope you will continue to use them throughout your studies and beyond.

© Chris McNulty 2017

9a. Preparation for Singing/Playing Tetrachords Over II-V-I-VI Progressions

*Track #12

Key of C

Chord: Dm7

Scale choices: D Dorian (*starting from the root*)
                         F Lydian (*starting from the min 3rd of the chord*)

Tetrachord: Minor I (*dorian*)   Minor I (*dorian*)

Piano short cut: Fmaj7/D

Chord: G7(b9)

Scale choice: Diminished (**half-whole**) *from Root*

Tetrachord: **Diminished**   **Diminished**

Piano short cut: F°7/G

Chord: Cmaj7(#11)

Scale choices: Lydian (*starting from root*)
                        Locrian (*starting from #11 of the chord*)

Tetrachord: **Whole tone** (*lydian*)   **Major**

Piano short cut: Em7/C

© Chris McNulty 2017

Chord: A+7(#9) (ALT)

Scale choices: **Altered** (*starting from the root*)
                             Lydian Augmented (*starting from the 3rd of chord*)

Tetrachord: **Diminished**   **Whole tone** (*lydian*)

Piano short cut: C#+maj7/A

Chord: Dm7

Scale choices: **D Dorian** (*starting from the root*)
                          F Lydian (*starting from the min 3rd of the chord*)

Tetrachord: **Minor I** (*dorian*)   **Minor I** (*dorian*)

Piano short cut: Fmaj7/D

Chord: G7(b9)

Scale choice: **Diminished (half-whole) from Root**

Tetrachord: **Diminished**   **Diminished**

Piano short cut: F°/G

Chord: Cmaj7(#11)

Scale Choice: Locrian (*starting from #11 of the chord*)
Lydian (*starting from root*)

Tetrachord: Minor II (*phrygian*)   Whole tone (*lydian*)

Piano short cut: Em9/C

(*passing chords to II of I in Key of F*)

Chord: Am9(add13)   Abm7   Abm7

Scale choices: A Dorian   Ab Dorian

melodising....

Piano short cut: Cmaj7(#11)/A   Bmaj7/Ab   Bmaj7/Ab

Key of F

Chord: Gm7

Scale choices: Bb Lydian (*starting from the min 3rd of the chord*)
G Dorian (*starting from the root*)

Tetrachord: Whole tone (*lydian*)   Major

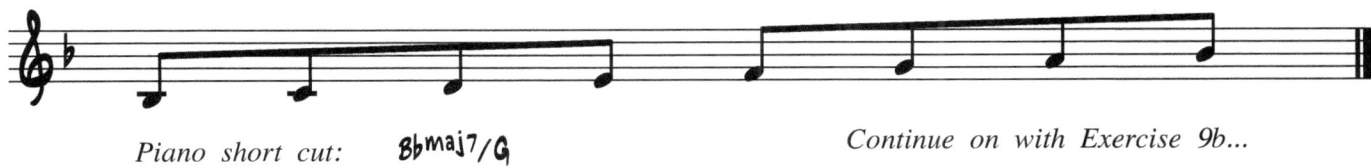

Piano short cut: Bbmaj7/G   *Continue on with Exercise 9b...*

Exercise 9b (tracks #12, #13) — Singing Scales using Tetrachords over II, V, I, VI progression through all 12 keys.

This exercise uses a **II, V, I, VI** progression to sing/play through all 12 keys. The term **"event"** is used to delineate each section where a new chord — scale — tetrachord occurs. This exercise moves in a cycle of 4th's through all 12 keys.

The 1st event of each key starts with the **II chord** and is straight out of the Major scale (2nd mode of Major - Dorian). Wherever I've delineated more than one scale choice you can start from either. On a Minor 7th chord you can use either **D Dorian or F Lydian**. They both sound equally good (make sure you utilize earlier exercises if you need further reinforcement).

The 2nd event uses a **V chord** with a slightly different quality to the V chord from the Major scale. I'm doing this so you have the opportunity to sing all six tetrachords as well as helping you integrate the sourcing and identifying of specific scales aurally and visually. This particular **Dom 7** chord has the qualities of a **b9, #9 and #11** and if you've been studying hard will know that this Dom7 chord sources to the **Diminished (half-whole) Scale** [*see Appendix 4, Chap 4 Ex.6*]. Both bookend tetrachords are Diminished (as delineated).

The 3rd event over the I chord is a Maj 7 chord but this time with the #11 quality. Use either the **Lydian** scale (staring from the root) - **Tetrachords: Whole tone** (*lydian*)**, Major** or **Locrian (b2)** (starting from the # 11) - Tetrachords - **Minor II** (*phrygian*)**, Whole tone** (*lydian*) [*See Appendix 5*].

The 4th event is a choice I made because in jazz the VI chord (6th mode of the Major scale - Aeolian) is often substituted with the **Augmented Dom 7 chord** (7th mode of Melodic minor scale) using the **Altered scale - Tetrachords: Diminished, Whole tone** (*lydian*). [*See Chapter 3, Ex.5a, b*]

The 5th, 6th & 7th events return to the **II, V, I** progression.

The 8th event sees the appearance of the standard **VI** chord proceeding to a 1/2 step movement to the next key event. I've created several different motifs, which fit with each of the two chords in Bar 8. I arrived at the melodies by ear, however if you want to see the theory behind it, take a look at the piano short-cuts (chord voicings). Whenever a Sus7 voicing is used I'm singing a 9th to 13th in the melody. When I'm using a minor chord voicing my melody starts on the minor 3rd of the chord

The 9th event is a resting bar for the 1/2 step motion however, at measure 27 I start introducing a lick to lead me to the first note of the next key. It's a **Minor II** (*phrygian*) tetrachord sung up and then down leading in 1/2 step motion to the tonic (root) of the II chord in the new key. It's cool to see just how much we sing these naturally. I've included this lick/melody in the 9th measure for several consecutive events but also left others blank so you can sing them yourself. Singers with natural hearing ability will internalize and sing these fairly easily BUT remember to find your own too. Just remember the trick is to land a 1/2 step away from the first note of the II chord in the next key. Ear singers will find this naturally once they have heard it a few times.

This pattern is constant except for two event modifications. The first modification is introduced at **Bar 53** where the **Sus7 chord** substitutes the standard **VI** chord. **Sus7 chords** and **VI chord**s are interchangeable when moving from certain key centers. The chord voicing/short cut is delineated as **AbMaj7/Bb**. Keep your ears open as I change the motif. Instead of singing a melody I sing the tension tones of the Sus7 chord. That pattern continues mostly through to the end. This only ever happens in the 8th measure of each key event. Isolating the tension tones clearly demonstrates that the event has been modified. I also use a different lick to hook up to the next key. In this instance I sing a **Minor I** (*dorian*) **tetrachord** up to the 5th and back down to lead me in 1/2 step motion to the II chord of the next key. Check the theory after you hear it naturally first. If it happens naturally great but if not, go sit at the piano and find something. Keep in mind that the note you end up on when singing a hook up lick to the next key needs to be a 1/2 step from the root of the II chord.

The only other chord/scale event modification happens at **measure 88 (at the 6th event)** and continues to occur at the 6th event to the end of the exercise. This event modification introduces a different quality of **Dom7** chord, one with the quality of **b9, b13**. It replaces the **Dom7 b9 #11 chord**. This new V chord sources to the **5th mode of Harmonic Minor - the Arabic scale** (*see Chapter 3 Ex.4, Ex 5c and Appendix 2*). This is where we finally get to sing the Harmonic tetrachord across moving harmony. Remember this one has the minor 3rd interval.

*** Please note that the Dom 7 chord has the most diverse number of qualities and therefore the most functionality out of all the chord types. To help assist you with which scales source to each of quality of Dom 7 chord [*See Appendix 1, 2, & 3*].

The tracks provided for this exercise are at a slower tempo because there are so few resting bars. As singers we need time for breath as well as for the challenge of accurate pitching. I'd therefore suggest leaving the first note off a tetrachord every so often to allow time for breath. I've included one slow/medium swing track and one slow bossa nova track for a little variety.

**** You will notice that in some instances I've begun a scale or tetrachord using a tension tone. I've done this to best explain the theory behind Derivative and Parallel use. However, whenever possible throughout these exercises, after you've integrated the theory, I suggest you use your ears and choose a chord tone to pivot your first note from.

9b. Using Tetrachords to Sing/Play Scales over II-V-I-VI Progressions

*Track #13, 14, 15

Key of C

Chord: Dm7   G7(b9)

Scale choice: D Dorian or F Lydian   G Diminished (Half-whole) from root

Tetrachord: Minor I (*dorian*)   Minor I (*dorian*)   Diminished   Diminished

Piano short cut: Fmaj7/D   F°7/G

Chord: Cmaj7(#11)   A+7(#9) ALT

Scale choice: C Lydian (*starting from root*) or   A Altered (*starting from the root*) or
F# Locrian (*starting from #11*)   Db Lydian Augmented (*starting from the 3rd*)

Tetrachords: Whole tone (*lydian*)   Major   Diminished   Lydian

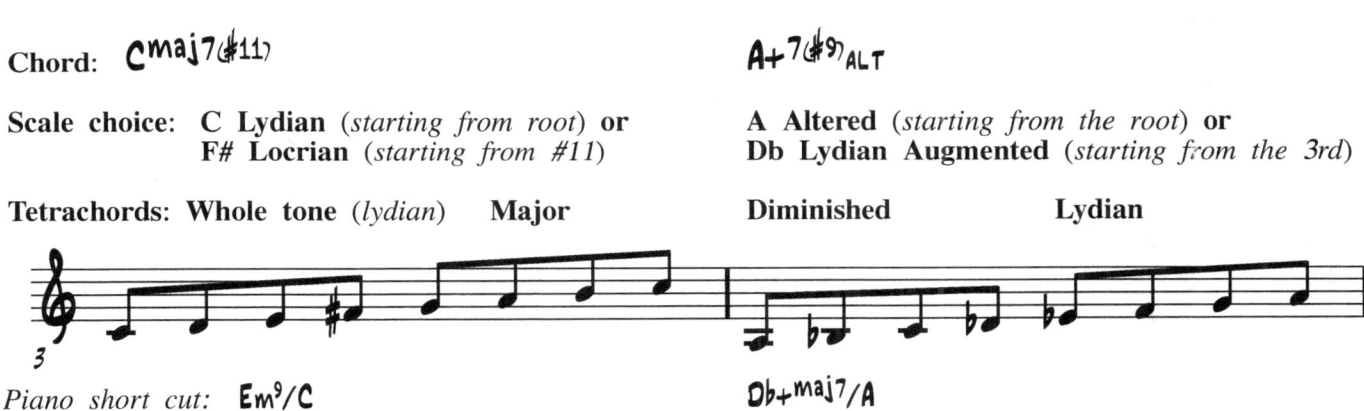

Piano short cut: Em9/C   Db+maj7/A

Chord: Dm7   G7(b9)

Scale Choice: D Dorian   G Diminished (Half-whole) from root

Tetrachord: Minor I (*dorian*)   Minor (*dorian*)   Diminished   Diminished

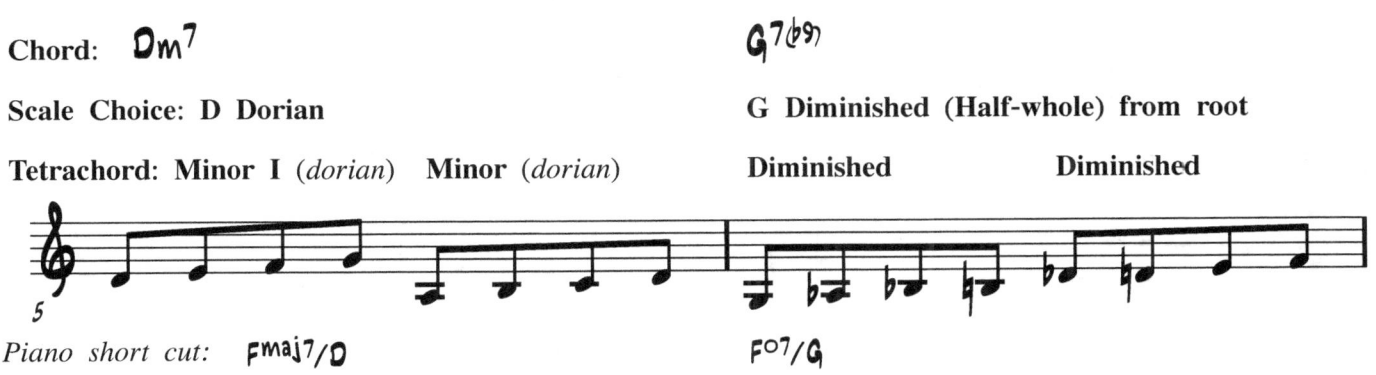

Piano short cut: Fmaj7/D   F°7/G

© Chris McNulty 2017

(passing chords to II of I in Key of F)

Chords: Cmaj7(#11)   Am9   Abm9   Abm9

Scale choice: C Lydian *(starting from #11)*   A Dorian   Ab Dorian
    or F# Locrian *(starting from root)*

Tetrachords:
    Minor II *(phrygian)*   Whole tone *(lydian)*

Piano short cut: Em9/C   Cmaj7/A   Bmaj7/Ab   Bmaj7/Ab

Key of F

Chord: Gm7   C7(b9)

Scale choice: G Dorian or Bb Lydian   C Diminished (Half-whole) from root

Tetrachord: Minor I *(dorian)* Minor I *(dorian)*   Diminished   Diminished

Piano short cut: Bbmaj7/G   Bb°7/C

Chord: Fmaj7(#11)   D+7(#9) ALT

Scale choice: F Lydian *(starting from root)* or   D Altered *(starting from the root)* or
    B Locrian *(starting from #11)*   Lydian Augmented *(starting from the 3rd)*

Tetrachords: Whole tone *(lydian)* Major   Diminished   Whole tone *(lydian)*

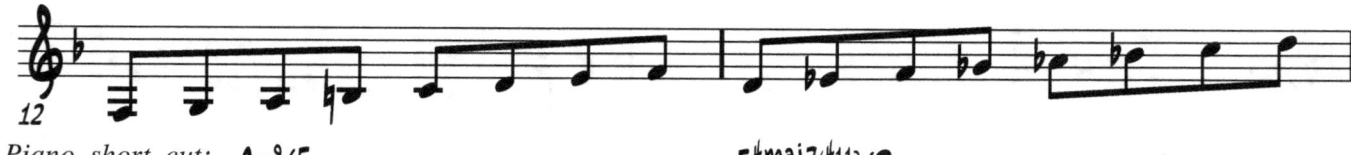

Piano short cut: Am9/F   F#maj7(#11)/D

© Chris McNulty 2017

Chord: Gm7   C7(b9)

Scale Choice: G Dorian or Bb Lydian   C Diminished (Half-whole) from root

Tetrachord: Minor I (*dorian*)   Minor (*dorian*)   Diminished   Diminished

Piano short cut: Bbmaj7/G   Bbº7/C

(*passing chords to II of I in Key of Bb*)

Chords: Fmaj7(#11)   Dm9   Dbm9   Dbm9

Scale choice: F Lydian (*starting from #11*)   D Dorian   Db Dorian
       or   B Locrian (*starting from root*)

Tetrachords:
     Minor II (*phrygian*)   Whole tone

Piano short cut: Am9/F   Fmaj7/D   Emaj7/Db   Emaj7/Db

Key of Bb

Chord: Cm7   F7(b9)

Scale choice: C Dorian or Ab Lydian   Diminished (Half-whole) from root

Tetrachords: Minor I   Minor I   Diminished   Diminished

Piano short cut: Ebmaj7/C   Ebº7/F

Chord: **Bbmaj7(#11)** G+7(#9) ALT

Scale choice: **Bb Lydian** (*starting from root*) or **G Altered** (*starting from the root*) or
E Locrian (*starting from #11*) **Lydian Augmented** (*starting from the 3rd*)

Tetrachords: Whole tone   Major   Diminished   Whole tone (*lydian*)

Piano short cut: Dm9/Bb   Bmaj7(#11)/G

Chord: **Cm7**   F7(b9)

Scale: C Dorian or Eb Lydian   Diminished (Half-whole) from root

Tetrachord: Minor I (*dorian*)   Minor I (*dorian*)   Diminished   Diminished

Piano short cut: Ebmaj7/C   Eb°7/F

(*passing chords to II of I in key of E flat*)

Chords: **Bbmaj7(#11)**   **Gm9**   **Gbm9**   **Gbm9**

Scale choice:
Bb Lydian (*starting from root*)   **G Dorian**   **Gb Dorian**
or **E Locrian** (*starting from #11*)

Tetrachords:
Whole tone (*lydian*) Major

Introducing lick over Gb Dorian leading to starting note "F" of next Key Eb (melody is an Ab phrygian tetrachord)

Piano short cut: Dm9/Bb   Bbmaj7/G   Amaj7/Gb   Amaj7/Gb

© Chris McNulty 2017

Key of Eb

Chords: Fm7   Bb7(b9)

Scale choice: F Dorian or Ab Lydian   Diminished (Half-whole) from root

Tetrachords: Minor I (*dorian*)   **Minor I** (*dorian*)   **Diminished**   **Diminished**

Piano short cut: Abmaj7/F   Bo7/Bb

Chord: Ebmaj7(#11)   C+7(#9) ALT

Scale choice: Eb Lydian (*starting from the root*) **or**   C Altered (*starting from the root*) **or**
A Locrian (*starting from the #11*)   Lydian Augmented (*starting from the 3rd*)

Tetrachords: Minor II (*phrygian*)   **Whole tone**   **Diminished**   **Whole tone** (*lydian*)

Piano short cut: Gm9/Eb   Emaj7(#11)/C

Chord: Fm7   Bb7(b9)

Scale choice: F Dorian or Ab Lydian   Diminished (Half-whole) from root

Tetrachords: Minor I (*dorian*)   **Minor I** (*dorian*)   **Diminished**   **Diminished**

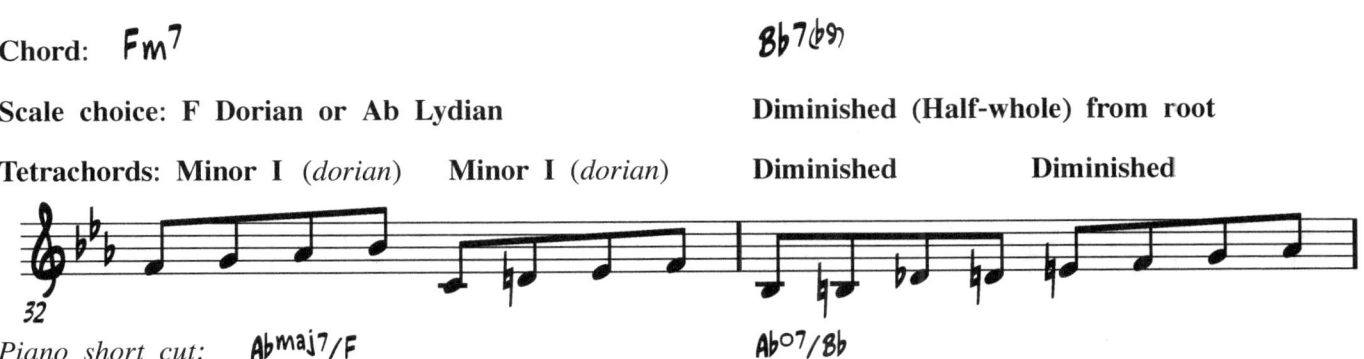

Piano short cut: Abmaj7/F   Abo7/Bb

© Chris McNulty 2017

(passing chords to II of I in key of A flat major)

Chords: Ebmaj7(#11)   Cm7   Bm9   Bm9

Scale choice:
  Eb Lydian *(starting from #11)*   C Dorian   B Dorian
or **A Locrian** *(starting from root)*

Tetrachords:
  Minor II *(dorian)* Whole tone *(lydian)*

*** lick is C# phrygian tetrachord

Piano short cut: Gm9/Eb   Ebmaj7/C   Dmaj7/B   Dmaj7/B

Key of Ab

Chords: Bbm7   Eb7(b9)

Scale choice: Bb Dorian or Db Lydian   Diminished (Half-whole) from root

Tetrachords: Minor I *(dorian)*   Minor I *(dorian)*   Diminished   Diminished

Piano short cut: Dbmaj7/Bb   Dbo7/Eb

Chords: Abmaj7(#11)   F+7(#9)ALT

Scale choice: **Ab Lydian** *(starting from root)* or   **F Altered** *(starting from the root)* or
  D Locrian *(starting from #11)*   **Lydian Augmented** *(starting from 3rd)*

Tetrachords: Whole tone *(lydian)* Major   Diminished   Whole tone *(lydian)*

Piano short cut: Cm9/Ab   Amaj7(#11)/F

© Chris McNulty 2017

Chord: **Bb m7**   **Eb7(b9)**

Scale choice: Bb Dorian or Db Lydian   Diminished (Half-whole) from root

Tetrachords: Minor I   Minor I   Diminished   Diminished

Piano short cut: **Dbmaj7/Bb**   **Db°7/Eb**

                                                                                                     (passing chords to next key of Db)

Chords: **Abmaj7(#11)**   **Fm9**   **Em9**   **Em9**

Scale choice:
    Ab Lydian *(starting from root)*   F Dorian   E Dorian
or   D Locrian *(starting from #11)*

Tetrachords: Whole tone   Major

                                                                   *** lick is F# phrygian tetrachord

Piano short cut:
    Cm9/Ab   **Abmaj7/F**   **Gmaj7/E**   **Gmaj7/E**

Key of Db

Chords: **Ebm7**   **Ab7(b9)**

Scale choice: Eb Dorian or Gb Lydian   Diminished (Half-whole) from root

Tetrachords: Minor I *(dorian)*   Minor I *(dorian)*   Diminished   Diminished

Piano short cut: **Gbmaj7/Eb**   **Gb°7/Ab**

© Chris McNulty 2017

Chords: D♭maj7(♯11)   B♭+7(♯9) ALT

Scale choice: **Db Lydian** (*starting from root*) **or**   **Bb Altered** (*starting from the root*) **or**
               G Locrian (*starting from #11*)   **Lydian Augmented** (*starting from the 3rd*)

Tetrachords: Whole tone (*lydian*)   Major   Diminished   Whole (*lydian*

Piano short cut: Fm9/Db   Dmaj7(♯11)/Bb

Chords: E♭m7   A♭7(♭9)

Scale choice: **Eb Dorian or   Gb Lydian**   **Diminished (Half-whole) from root**

Tetrachords: Minor I (*dorian*)   Minor I (*dorian*)   Diminished   Diminished

Piano short cut: Gbmaj7/Eb   Gb°7/Ab

                                                                     (*passing chords to II of I in Key of Gb Major*)

Chords: D♭maj7(♯11)   B♭7(sus4)   Am9   Am9

Scale choice:
    Db Lydian (*starting from root*)   **Bb Dorian   A Dorian**
 or **G Locrian** (*starting from #11*)

Tetrachords:
            Whole tone   Major   *Tension tones*   *Chord tones*

Piano short cut: Fm9/Db   Abmaj7/Bb   Cmaj7/A   Cmaj7/A

© Chris McNulty 2017

Key of Gb

Chords: Abm7   Db7(b9)

Scale choice: Ab Dorian or B Lydian   Diminished (Half-whole) from root

Tetrachords: Minor I (*dorian*)   Minor I (*dorian*)   Diminished   Diminished

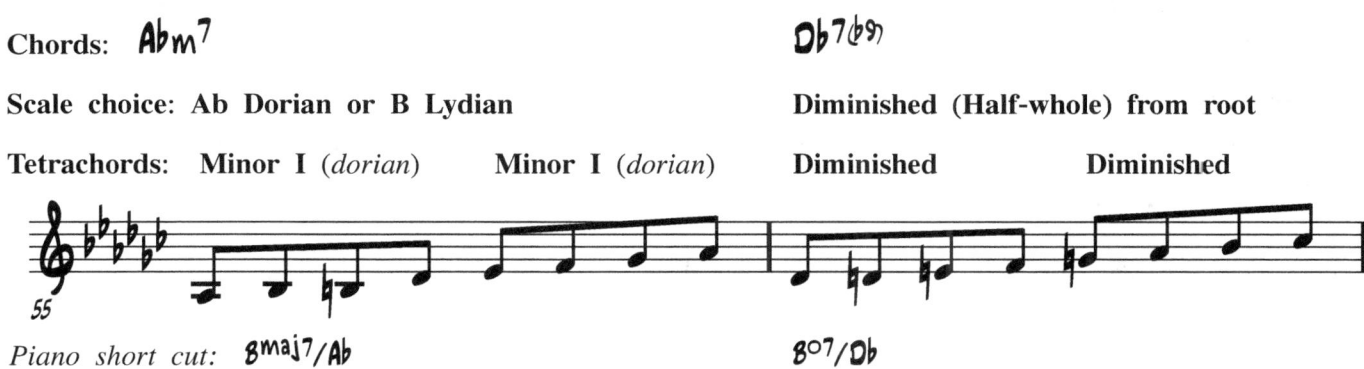

Piano short cut: Bmaj7/Ab   B°7/Db

Chords: Gbmaj7(#11)   Eb+7(#9) ALT

Scale choice: Gb Lydian (*starting from root*) or   Eb Altered (*starting from the root*) or
C Locrian (*starting from #11*)   Lydian Augmented (*starting from the 3rd*)

Tetrachords: Whole tone (*lydian*)   Major   Diminished   Whole tone

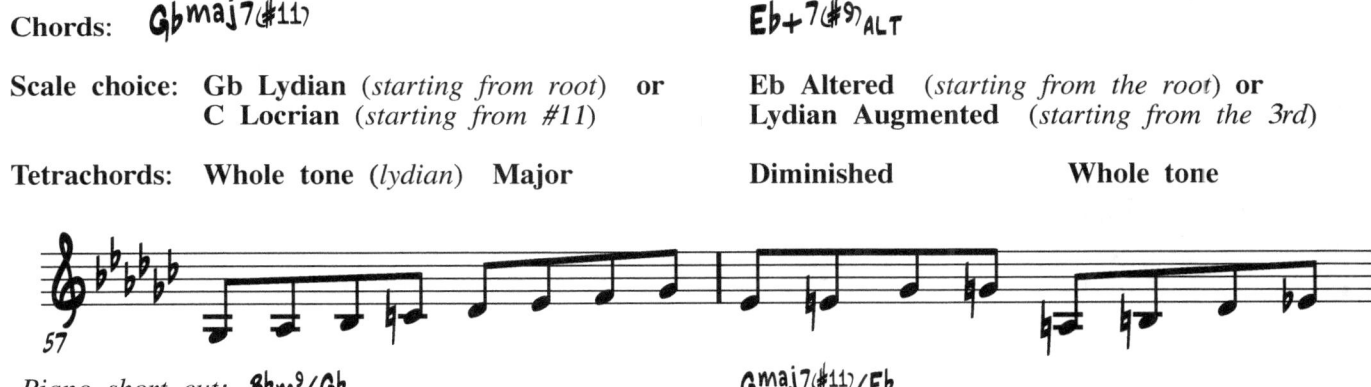

Piano short cut: Bbm9/Gb   Gmaj7(#11)/Eb

Chords: Abm7   Db7(b9)

Scale choice: Ab Dorian   B Lydian   Diminished (Half-whole) from root

Tetrachords: Minor I (*dorian*)   Minor I   Diminished   Diminished

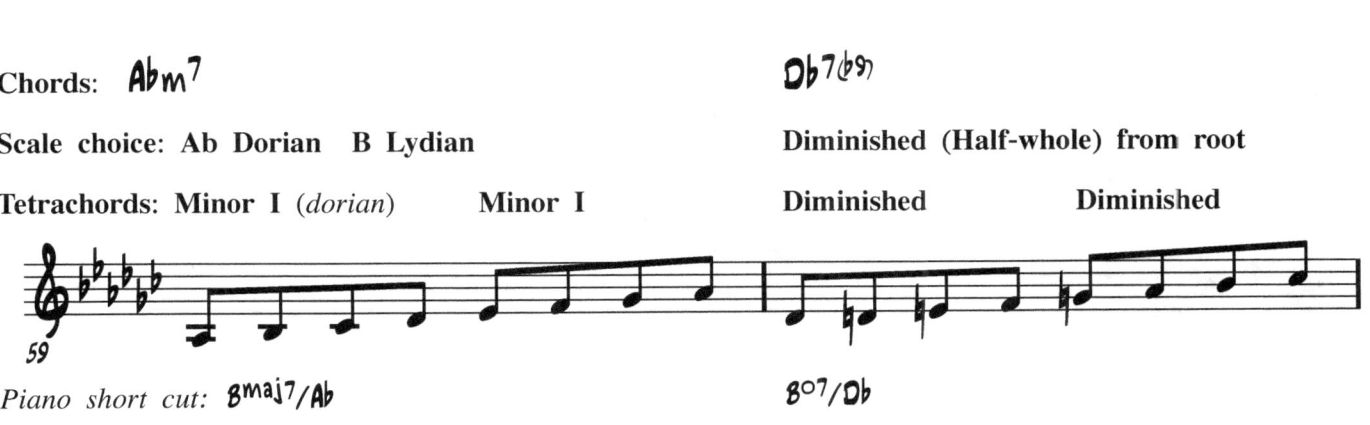

Piano short cut: Bmaj7/Ab   B°7/Db

© Chris McNulty 2017

(passing chords to II of I in Key of B major)

Chords: Gbmaj7(#11)　　　　　　　Ebm7　　　Dm9　　　Dm9

Scale choice:
　　Gb Lydian *(starting from root)*　　　　Eb Dorian　　D Dorian
or　C Locrian *(starting from #11)*

Tetrachords: Whole tone　　Major

Piano short cut: Bbm9/Gb　　　　　Gbmaj7(#11)/Eb　　Fmaj7/D　　Fmaj7/D

Key of B

Chords: C#m7　　　　　　　　　　　　F#7(b9)

Scale choice: C# Dorian or E Lydian　　　Diminished (Half-whole) from root

Tetrachords: Minor I *(dorian)*　　Minor I　　Diminished　　Diminished

Piano short cut: Emaj7/C#　　　　　　　　Eo7/F#

Chords: Bmaj7(#11)　　　　　　　　　　G#+7(#9) ALT

Scale choice: B Lydian *(starting from root)* or　　G# Altered *(starting from the root)* or
　　F Locrian *(starting from #11*　　　　　　Lydian Augmented *(starting from the 3rd)*

Tetrachords: Whole *(lydian)*　　Major　　Diminished　　Whole tone

Piano short cut: D#m9/B　　　　　　　Cmaj7#11/G#

© Chris McNulty 2017

Play Arabic starting from the root (Parallel)
Play Harmonic Minor starting from the 4th

Chords: C#m7   F#7(b9)

Scale choice: C# Dorian or E Lydian   Arabic (5th mode of Harmonic Minor)

Tetrachords: Minor I (*dorian*)   Minor I   Harmonic   Minor II (*phrygian*)

Piano short cut: Emaj7(#11)/C#   E°7/F#

(passing chord to II of E major)

Chords: Bmaj7(#11)   G#m9   Gm9   Gm9

Scale choice:
  B Lydian (*starting from root*)   G# Dorian   G Dorian
  or F Locrian (*starting from #11*)

Tetrachords: Whole tone   Major

*** lick is an "A phrygian" tetrachord

Piano short cut: D#m9/B   Bmaj7/G#   Bbmaj7/G   Bbmaj7/G

Key of E

Chords: F#m7   B7(b9)

Scale choice: F# Dorian or A Lydian   Diminished (Half-whole) from root

Tetrachords: Minor I (*dorian*)   Minor I   Diminished   Diminished

Piano short cut: Amaj7/F#   A°7/B

Chords: **Emaj7(#11)**   **C#+7(#9)ALT**

Scale choice: **E Lydian** (*starting from root*) or   **C# Altered** (*starting from the root*) or
A# Locrian (*starting from #11*)   **Lydian Augmented** (*starting from the 3rd*)

Tetrachords: Whole tone   Major   Diminished   Whole tone

Piano short cut: **G#m9/E**   **Fmaj7(#11)/C#**

Chords: **F#m7**   **B7(b9)**

Scale choice: **F# Dorian** or **A Lydian**   **Arabic** (5th mode of Harmonic Minor)

Tetrachords: Minor I (*dorian*)   Minor I   Harmonic   Minor II (*phrygian*)

Piano short cut: **Amaj7(#11)/F#**   **A°7/B**

(*passing chords to II of I in key of A major*)

Chords: **Emaj7(#11)**   **C#(sus4)**   **Cm9**   **Cm9**

Scale choice:
E Lydian (*starting from root*)   **C# Dorian**   **C Dorian**
or **A# Locrian** (*starting from #11*)

Tetrachords:
Whole tone   Major   *Tension tones*   *Chord tones*

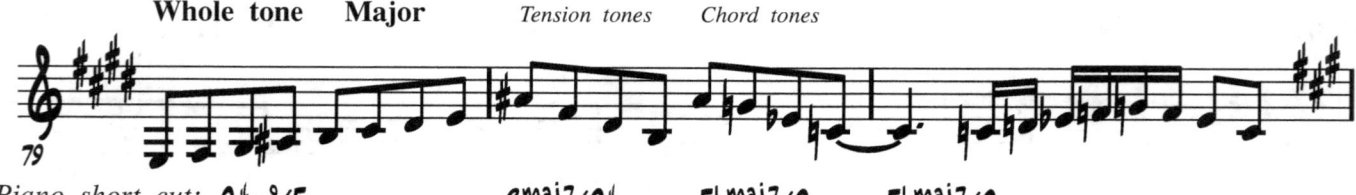

Piano short cut: **G#m9/E**   **Bmaj7/C#**   **Ebmaj7/C**   **Ebmaj7/C**

Key of A

Chords: Bm⁹   E7(♭9)

Scale choice: B Dorian or D Lydian   Diminished (Half-whole) from root

Tetrachords: Minor I *(dorian)*   Minor I   Diminished   Diminished

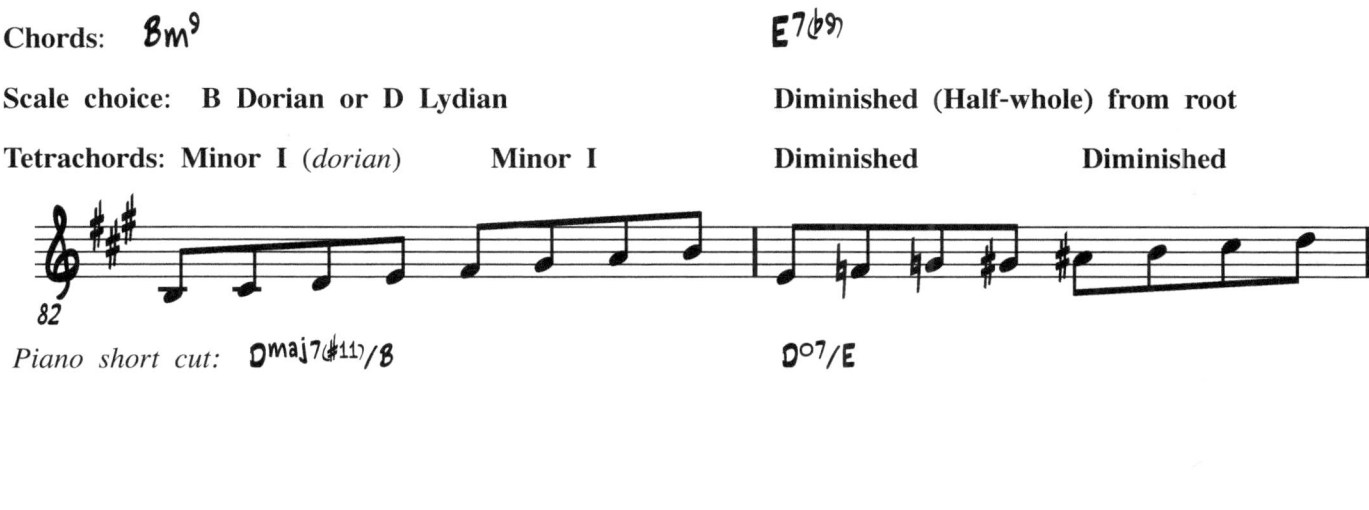

Piano short cut: Dmaj7(#11)/B   D°7/E

Chords: Amaj7(#11)   F#+7(#9) ALT

Scale choice: A Lydian *(starting from root)* or   F# Altered *(starting from the root)* or
                  D# Locrian *(starting from #11)*   Lydian Augmented *(starting from the 3rd)*

Tetrachords:
          Whole tone *(lydian)*   Major   Diminished   Whole tone

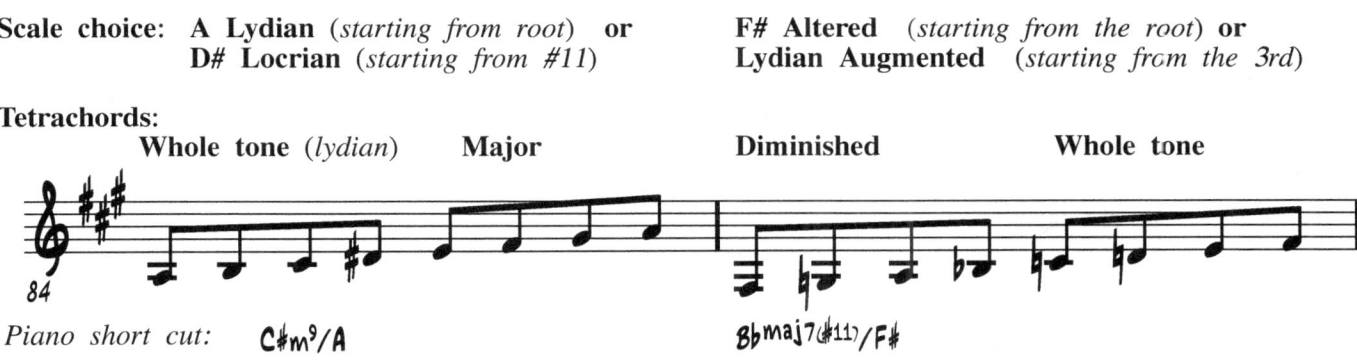

Piano short cut: C#m⁹/A   B♭maj7(#11)/F#

Chords: Bm⁹   E7(♭9)

Scale choice: B Dorian or D Lydian   Arabic (5th Mode of Harmonic Minor)

Tetrachords: Minor I *(dorian)*   Minor I   Harmonic   Minor II *(phrygian)*

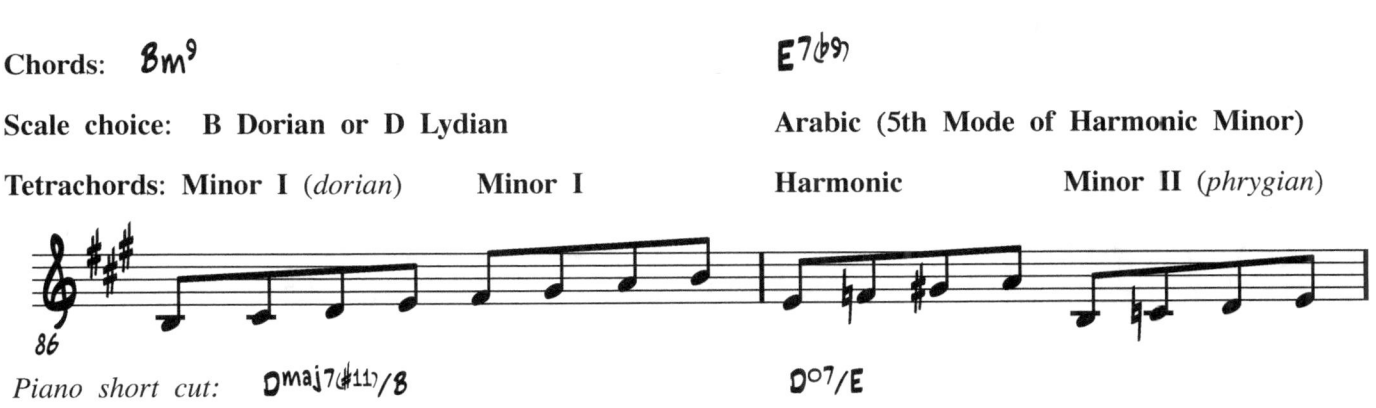

Piano short cut: Dmaj7(#11)/B   D°7/E

© Chris McNulty 2017

(passing chord to II of I in D Maj)

Chords: Amaj7(#11)   F#(sus4)   Fm9   Fm9

Scale choice:
A Lydian *(starting from root)*   F# Dorian   F Dorian
or D# Locrian *(starting from #11)*

Tetrachords:
   Whole tone   Major   *Tension tones*   *Chord tones*

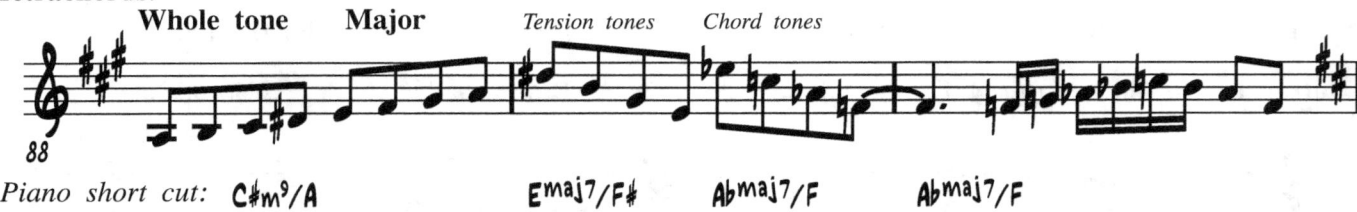

Piano short cut: C#m9/A   Emaj7/F#   Abmaj7/F   Abmaj7/F

Key of D

Chords: Em7   A7(b9)

Scale choice: E Dorian or G Lydian   Diminished (Half-whole) from root

Tetrachords: Minor I *(dorian)*   Minor I   Diminished   Diminished

Piano short cut: Gmaj7/E   G°7/A

Chords: Dmaj7(#11)   B#+7(#9)ALT

Scale choice: D Lydian *(starting from root)* or   B Altered *(starting from the root)* or
   G# Locrian *(starting from #11)*   Lydian Augmented *(starting from the 3rd)*

Tetrachords:
   Whole tone *(lydian)*   Major   Diminished   Whole tone

Piano short cut: F#m9/D   Ebmaj7(#11)/B

© Chris McNulty 2017

Chords: Em7 A7(b9)

Scale choice: E Dorian or G Lydian   Arabic (5th Mode of Harmonic Minor)

Tetrachords: Minor I (*dorian*)   Minor I   Harmonic   Minor II (*phrygian*)

Piano short cut: Gmaj7(#11)/E   G°7/A

(passing chords to II of I of G major)

Chords: Dmaj7(#11)   B(sus4)   Bbm9   Bbm9

Scale choice:
  D Lydian (*starting from root*)   B Dorian   Bb Dorian
  or G# Locrian (*starting from #11*)

Tetrachords:
  Whole tone   Major   *Tension tones*   *Chord tones*

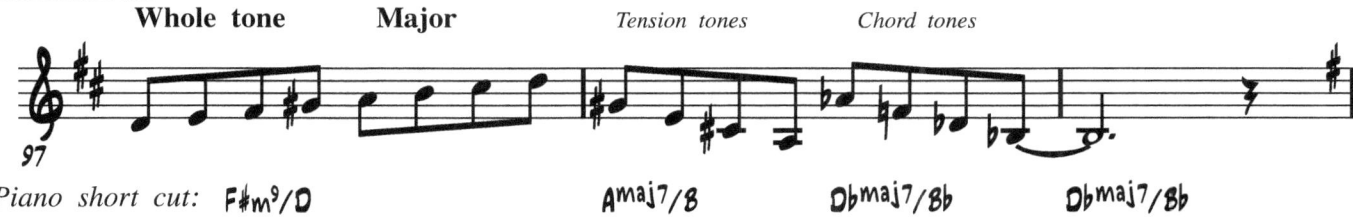

Piano short cut: F#m9/D   Amaj7/B   Dbmaj7/Bb   Dbmaj7/Bb

Key of G

Chords: Am7   D7(b9)

Scale choice: A Dorian or C Lydian   Diminished (Half-whole) from root

Tetrachords: Minor I (*dorian*)   Minor I   Diminished   Diminished

Piano short cut: Cmaj7/A   C°7/D

© Chris McNulty 2017

Chords: G maj7(#11)　　　　　　　　　　　　　　E+7(#9) ALT

Scale choice: G Lydian (*starting from root*) or　　E Altered (*starting from the root*) or
C# Locrian (*starting from #11*)　　　　　　　Lydian Augmented (*starting from the 3rd*)

Tetrachords: Whole tone (*lydian*)　Major　　　Diminished　　　Whole tone

Piano short cut: Bm9/G　　　　　　　　　　　Abmaj7(#11)/E

Chords: Am7　　　　　　　　　　　　　　　D7(b9)

Scale choice: A Dorian or C Lydian　　　　Arabic (5th Mode of Harmonic Minor)

Tetrachords:
　　Minor I (*dorian*)　　Minor I　　　Harmonic　　Minor II (*phrygian*)

Piano short cut: Cmaj7(#11)/A　　　　　　　C°7/D

　　　　　　　　　　　　　　　　　　　　　　(*passing chord to II of I in C major*)

Chords: Gmaj7(#11)　　　　E(sus4)　　Ebm9　　Ebm9

Scale choice:
　G Lydian (*starting from root*)　　E Dorian　　Eb Dorian
or C# Locrian (*starting from #11*)

Tetrachords:
　　Whole tone　Major　　*Tension tones*　*Chord tones*

Piano short cut: Bm9/G　　　Dmaj7/E　　Gbmaj7/Eb　　Gbmaj7/Eb

Chapter Seven - Soloing over "Softly" chord changes

Exercise 10a — Warming Up (track #14)

These warm ups are a good way to prepare for many tunes. I've incorporated most of the changes that appear in "Softly" as well as a few extras thrown in for good measure. The explanations below refer to each four bar event, unless otherwise noted. In all instances the chord will be heard first followed by my voice outlining the chord and tension tones, followed by the tetrachords (1/4 notes and then 1/8th notes). At the end of each exercise the chords are repeated without my voice to give you an opportunity to sing the shapes independently.

> **The first event** (first four measures) are basic triads to help you get used to pitching major, augmented (#5), minor and diminished chords. Don't focus too much on "why am I singing these"? The main point to these kinds of warms ups is to open your ears up to hearing and pitching. In this exercise I'm outlining four different triad shape qualities.

> *** *A Triad = 3 notes: 1, 3, 5 with either chord tone flattened or sharpened (except the root of course). By **Chord tone we mean** (1, 3, 5, 7). By **Tension tone we mean** 2 (9), 4 (11), 6 (13). Outside of the tonic or root these chord and tension tones can be either flattened, raised natural (or perfect).*

> **The 2nd and 3rd four bar events** outline (1) a **Major 7th** chord singing chord and tension tones (up and down the scale) moving to an **Augmented 7th** chord (this progression appears in the first 2 bars of the bridge) and (2) a **Minor chord** moving to a 1/2 **Diminished** chord [*the first 2 bars of the song*].

> **The 4th event** outlines the **Maj 7th #11** chord singing chord and tension tones. From this event onwards in addition to the chord and tension tones I bring in the tetrachord shapes. Starting on the tonic of the chord you sing/play a **Whole tone** (*Lydian*) followed by a **Major** tetrachord. When singing the scale downwards from the 9th (depending on which quality of 9th it is) I choose a **Minor I** followed by a **Major** tetrachord. Experiment and find your own way back down the scale from any starting note above the octave. Identify what two tetrachords you are singing.

> **The 5th event** introduces the **Augmented Maj 7** chord (+Maj7). Again outlining both chord and tension tones followed by the tetrachords. When singing the **Lydian Augmented** scale we use **Whole tone** (*Lydian*) followed

© Chris McNulty 2017

by a **Diminished** tetrachord. When singing down from the 9th I chose **Minor I** followed by a **Whole tone** tetrachord. To give you a little extra time to hear the scale (using tetrachords) I've included 2 bars of 1/4 notes repeated by 2 bars of 1/8th notes.

The 6th event introduces the **Augmented Dom 7 #9** chord. The information provided on the stave is there to assist. Look at it carefully. When singing the **Altered Scale** we sing/play a **Diminished** followed by a **Whole tone** (*lydian*) tetrachord. When singing the scale downwards from the #9 I choose **Minor I** (*dorian*) followed by a **Minor II** (*phrygian*) tetrachord.

The 7th event brings us back to a standard minor chord outlining chord, tension tones and tetrachords.

10a. Warm Ups for Soloing

*Start with Simple Triads

*Then outline chord tones of Major, Augmented, Minor and Diminished 7 chords

Chord: Cmaj7(#11)

Scale: Lydian (4th mode of Major scale)

Tetrachords: Whole tone (*lydian*)   Major

Chord: Cmaj7(#11)

Scale: Lydian (4th mode of Major scale)

Tetrachords: Whole tone (*lydian*)   Major   Minor I (*dorian*)   Major

Singing down from the 9th

Chord: C+maj7

Scale: Lydian Augmented (3rd mode of Melodic Minor)

Tetrachords: Whole tone (*lydian*) **Diminished**

Chord: C+maj7

Scale: Lydian Augmented (3rd mode of Melodic Minor)

Tetrachords: **Whole tone** (*lydian*) **Diminished**

Chord: C+maj7

Scale: Lydian Augmented (3rd mode of Melodic Minor)

Tetrachords: **Whole tone   Diminished   Minor I** (*dorian*) **Whole tone**

Sing/play scale down from the 9th

***Note: chord symbol for Augmented 7 chord indicates #5 (Altered scale infers (no 5th) b13

Chord: A+7(#9)

Scale: Altered Scale (Diminished/whole tone scale)

Tetrachords: **Diminished**   **Whole tone** (*lydian*)

© Chris McNulty 2017

Chord: A+7(#9)

Scale: Altered Scale (Diminished/whole tone scale)

Tetrachords: Diminished   Whole tone (*lydian*)

Chord: A+7(#9)

Scale: Altered Scale (Diminished/whole tone scale)

Tetrachords: Diminished   Whole tone (*lydian*)   Minor (*dorian*)   Minor II (*phrygian*)

Sing the Scale down from the 9th

Chord: Am7

Chord Tones   *Tension Tones*

Chord: Am7

Tetrachords: Minor I   Minor I

© Chris McNulty 2017   85

Exercise 10b — Preparing for improvising over "Softly" changes

The 8th event reinforces the theory behind derivative and parallel use and demonstrates how to utilize parallel and derivative scale choices. Please refer to [*Appendix 2 Chord-Scale Relationships (Parallel & Derivative uses)*].

I've purposely left the chord and tension tones out as you have already practiced them over the **A+7 #9 chord** in the **6th event**. For this event the focus is on tetrachord choices based on either singing the scale from the root of the chord (**Parallel**) or singing the **Parent scale** from a chord or tension tone (**Derivative**). Keep in mind the principle remains the same throughout all these exercises. In this instance whenever you see an **Augmented 7 #9 chord** you can either choose to hear/sing the **Altered scale** sung from the root of the chord OR you can choose to identify with the parent scale (**Melodic minor**) which with practice will always be located a 1/2 step up from the root of any **Augmented 7 #9 chord**. Remember the **Altered scale** sources to the 7th mode of Melodic minor.
Example: B Altered Scale sources to **C Melodic Minor**, a 1/2 step up from B (the root).

Once you've integrated **Chapters 1, 2 & 3** you'll have a better grasp of **Parallel** and **Derivative** use. To start with we first need to identify what mode of what scale the **Augmented 7** chord sources to. We know it's the 7th mode of Melodic Minor. What is E+7 #9 the 7th mode of? It has to be **F Melodic Minor.** Think up a minor 2nd (1/2 step). If you're not using the Parallel option (Altered scale) you're using some version of Derivative. All you need to make a decision about is the starting note. This is where ears count for everything and always over rule theory. The theory of scale usage/choices as you learned in the earlier exercises is first learned derivatively, however once the theory is integrated your best choice will be Parallel usage. This principle can be applied across all 12 keys. In this example whenever you hear/see an **+7#9 chord** you can sing the **Altered scale** (tetrachords: **Diminished, Whole tone**) starting of course from the root of the chord which in this instance is "E" OR you can source the parent scale, **F Melodic Minor.**

After hearing the chord shape the next two measures have you singing/playing a **Whole tone** (*Lydian*) tetrachord followed by a **Diminished** tetrachord starting on Ab (G#). This is Derivative sourcing using **F Melodic minor** but starting on the minor 3rd (Ab) (remember hearing/ears). *** Note pitched against E+7 #9 the Ab (G#) is the major 3rd. Once again I'm including tetrachords as 1/4 notes followed by 1/8th notes so you can get used to hearing the sound shapes.

© Chris McNulty 2017

We then switch to **Parallel** usage singing the **Altered scale** from the root of the chord. Sing/play a **Diminished** tetrachord followed by a **Whole tone** (*lydian*) tetrachord.

The 8th event is completed by referencing two different chord qualities. We clearly hear how the dots connect across harmonic passages. Play/sing "**E**" **Altered scale (Diminished, Whole tone** tetrachords) over **E+7#9** chord up to its octave to "**E**" which becomes the **5th** of **Amin7**. Pitching down from "**E**" to "**A**" using the Dorian scale. Combining scale and tetrachord morphs into melody.

As a separate exercise go to the piano. Play **E+7#9** or starting on any note and playing a chord of this quality. Voiced as follows:

> Left hand: Play **E** (an octave apart) **G#, D and G** (use the sustain pedal).
> Right hand: Play **F Melodic minor**.

First starting from the root "**F**" then start from "**G**" and then from "**Ab**" (**G#**). You'll soon hear how chord tones often make better choices to sing/play from than a tension tone when starting on strong beat.

This event starts off by going back to singing the chord and tension tones. Moving straight to Parallel usage singing the **Arabic scale** over the **A7b9 chord**. Remember, when using Parallel the scale is always sung/played from the root of the chord. The tetrachords for the **Arabic** scale are **Harmonic** followed by **Minor II** (*phrygian*). Moving to Derivative you will hear a very different sound. Remember we learn derivative use first. Which chord sources to which degree of the Parent scale (in this instance Harmonic). Whenever you see a **Dom 7** chord with the qualities of **b9, b13** you'll learn with practice that it sources to the **5th mode of Harmonic Minor**. In this instance A7b9,b13. "**A**" being the 5th of "**D**" implies the use of **D Harmonic minor**. Remember to use the Appendices. In this instance *Appendix 2. [Also refer to Harmonic Minor template in Chapter 4, Ex.4]*.

Keep in mind **Derivative** works best in helping you identify which scale a chord sources to. Once you integrate each degree you can confidently move to Parallel usage. When in doubt go to the piano and play/sing the parent scale first starting from the first degree and then continue from each degree of the scale. Identify the chord that sources to each scale degree. Play the chord (1 3, 5 7) in LH (using sustain pedal) and in the RH play the scale from each degree. Remember chord tone on the strong beats (1 & 3), tension tones on the 2 & 4. Starting on the 4th or 1/2 step from a chord tone rarely sounds good on a down beat. For instance when using **D Harmonic minor** (Derivative) to sing over **A7b9**, starting from "**D**" would clash with the C# (the 3rd). We learn the theory of this using **Derivative** however once this methodology is integrated you'll soon move to **Parallel**.

10b. Preparing to Sing Over the Harmony of "Softly"

Using **F Melodic Minor** over E+7#9

    Derivative: Play/Sing F Melodic Minor (*starting on "G#"*)
    ****see explanation on oppposite page*

    Parallel: Play/sing the Altered Scale (*starting from the Root "E"*)

Chord: E+7(#9)

Scale: Melodic Minor (*starting on the G#*)   **Derivative** (*Starting on "F" would clash with "E"*)

Tetrachords: **Whole Tone** (*lydian*)   **Diminished**

Tetrachords: **Whole Tone**   **Diminished**   **Minor I**   **Whole tone** (*lydian*)

Now try using the Altered scale (7th Degree of Melodic Minor) ****starting from the Root*

Chord: E+7(#9)

Scale: E Altered Scale (*starting on the root "E"*)

Tetrachords: **Diminished**   **Whole tone** (*lydian*)

© Chris McNulty 2017

Chord: E+7(#9) (resolving to the A Minor chord) Am7

Scale: **Altered Scale** (*starting on the root "E"*)

Tetrachords: **Diminished**   **Whole tone** (*lydian*)

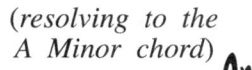

Working with the **"A Harmonic Minor"** scale over the following chord progression:

Am7   Bm7(b5)   E7

****Parent Scale at first degree is both Parallel and Derivative - Am(maj7)

Chord: Am(maj7)

Scale: **A Harmonic Minor**

Tetrachords: **Minor I** (*dorian*)   **Harmonic**

Chord: Am(maj7)

Scale: **A Harmonic Minor**

Tetrachords: **Minor I**   **Harmonic**   *** Non tetrachord occurance*   **Minor II** (*phrygian*)

Now try using it over these sets of changes

Chord: Am7   Bm7(b5)   E7

Scale: **A Harmonic Minor**

Tetrachords: **Minor I** (*dorian*)   **Harmonic**

© Chris McNulty 2017

Working with the "Arabic Scale" (5th degree of Harmonic Minor)

Remember this scale has the Harmonic Minor interval. At the 5th degree the harmonic interval occurs between the b9 and the Major 3rd

Chord: A7(b9)

Scale: Arabic: Root, b9, Maj 3rd, 11, 5, b13, b7

Parallel Use: "A" Arabic Scale (*from the root "A"*)

Derivative Use: "D" Harmonic Minor (*4th of the chord*)

Parallel Use: Sing/play the Arabic Scale (*starting from the Root "A"*)

Tetrachords: Harmonic   Minor II (*phyrgian*)

Derivative Use - Identify Parent scale - D Harmonic Minor

***BUT instead of starting on "D" start on "C#" as "D" would clash with the major 3rd (C#)

Tetrachords: Diminished   (*Non-tetrachord event*)

Chord: A7(b9)   A7(b9)

Scale: Harmonic Minor (starting from C#)   Arabic Scale (starting from the root "A")

Tetrachords: Diminished   ***non-tetrachord   Harmonic   Minor II (*phrygian*)

© Chris McNulty 2017

Completing the progression at the start of the Bridge in "Softly"

Chord: Cmaj7   A7(b9)

Scale: Lydian (Major)   D Harmonic Minor (starting from C#)

Tetrachords: Major   Minor I (*dorian*)   Diminished   *** *Non-tetrachord*

Chord: Cmaj7   A7(b9)

Scale: Lydian (Major)   Arabic (5th degree of Harmonic Minor)

Tetrachords: Major   Minor I (*dorian*)   Harmonic   Minor II (*phrygian*)

The 9th event utilizes the "**A**" **Harmonic minor** scale. Starting off with the chord that sources from the first degree - **Amin/maj7** and where Parallel and Derivative are always one and the same. This exercise shows you how to use Harmonic Minor over a completely different set of chord changes. We start off by singing the tetrachords that bookend **A Harmonic Minor** — **Minor I** (dorian) followed by a **Harmonic** over **Amin/maj7**. We then introduce a set of changes that appear throughout "Softly" — **Amin7, B 1/2 Diminished, E7**. Listen to how perfectly **A Harmonic Minor** works over that chord progression. Once you get familiar with this kind of usage look for it in other tunes/chord progressions. Try using different combinations of **Parallel** or **Derivative** scale use. For example take a look at "**Alone Together**" where you will find similar chord progressions.

> **The 10th event** introduces parallel use of **Harmonic Minor** using its 5th mode, the **Arabic Scale**. The chord that sources to the **Arabic Scale** is the **Dom7 b9, b13 chord**. Remember the Harmonic minor scale includes a minor 3rd interval. In jazz the Dom 7 chord has LOTS of functions. The choices an instrumentalist makes to choose one over the other is mostly connected to where one is traveling to or from harmonically, especially when it involves **II, V, I** movement through changing key centers.

We complete this exercise by finding **D Harmonic Minor's** use over a set of chord changes which appears at the opening of the bridge section of "Softly." Start by singing a simple major scale over two measures of **Cmaj7** followed by alternate movements from **Derivative to Parallel** over two measures of **A7b9**. By switching back and forth between **Derivative** use (**starting on the C#**) and **Parallel** use (singing the **Arabic scale** starting on "A") we not only hear how different each option sounds, but more importantly how singing two different combinations of tetrachords gives us two totally different but equally correct and great sounding outcomes.

Once you practice these warm ups you'll be ready to sing the solo I've created over the changes. Please note that in the soloing exercise (Ex.10c) I've indicated clearly above the stave whenever I'm using the Harmonic or Melodic minor scale (**Parallel or Derivative**). I've purposely not included all the choices I've outlined in Ex 10a and 10b. That would be overkill, however I hope I've given you some ideas for different approaches.

OK, now you're ready to use this method to improvise/solo over the changes to "Softly" in **Exercise 10c**. Sing along with my solo while looking at the information on the stave. Listen to how I start moving things around. Practice with me first then without me. Then try improvising your own!

10c. Soloing Over the Changes of "Softly"

*Tracks #17 - 20

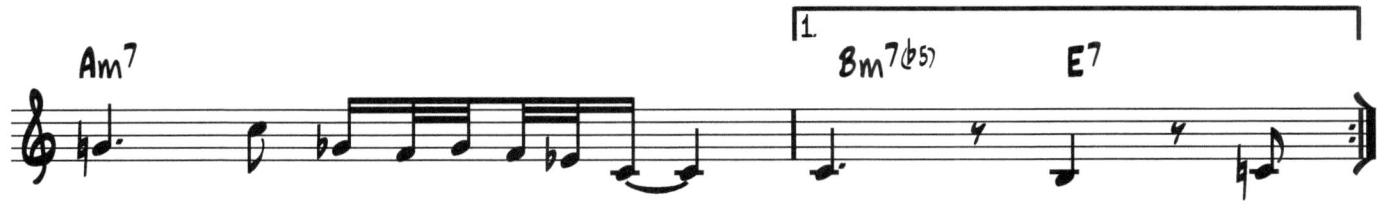

I'm starting my melody using notes from D Harmonic Minor starting on C# - Why? Use ears

Here's the A Harmonic Minor scale again

Chapter Eight — Pentatonic Scale uses — Major and Minor

The last exercises in this series gives you a break from tetrachords. Yay! It involves working with the Pentatonic scale (major-minor) and finding its uses over **Dom7 Sus chords, Augmented 7 chords, Minor 7 and Major 7 chords**.

Jazz instrumentalists have been incorporating pentatonic scale use into their melodic motifs and soloing explorations and compositions since the very early days of jazz, drawing from the blues. John Coltrane used them extensively. As vocalists we've also been hearing and using these scales, perhaps not in the same manner as jazz instrumentalists, nevertheless we've been hearing and singing them for a long time.

I've developed a few simple exercises which vocalists might find useful when incorporating pentatonic scales into their improvisations.

Exercise 11a (Template A) is your source document. Use this to assist you in understanding how these scales work over certain chord qualities. **Exercise 11b (Template B)** includes exercises which work over a specific set of chord changes. The harmonic passage I'm using is an excerpt from the vamp ending of an original composition of mine, **New Day** (Chris McNulty - Melody/Lyric, **Paul Bollenback** - harmony). [*Use Appendix 7 as a reference tool*].

The **Pentatonic scale is a 5 note scale** and is deeply rooted in the folk music of diverse and ancient cultures around the world. Its history and influence on those cultures and their music is significant. Instruments from Ethiopia to Indonesia are tuned to certain pentatonic scales. Over the centuries the pentatonic scale has found its way into classical harmony and composition. Both major and minor pentatonic scales are used by jazz musicians and their use has had a profound impact on jazz improvisation. Mainly because the scales work so well over certain harmonic passages. The blues scale is also predominantly derived from the minor pentatonic scale.

Exercise 11a — Pentatonic Scale-Chord Use (track #17)

C Major Pentatonic uses the same notes as **A Minor Pentatonic** (its relative minor pentatonic). This rule applies across all keys. **F Major Pentatonic** uses the same notes as **D Minor Pentatonic** and so on and so forth.

C Major Pentatonic Scale uses the following intervallic scale structure and notes: **Whole step, Whole step, Minor 3rd, Whole step, Minor 3rd**: C, D, E, G, A, C

A Minor Pentatonic Scale uses exactly the same notes, starting on "A" of the scale, creating a different intervallic scale structure: **Minor 3rd, Whole step, Whole step, Minor 3rd, Whole step**: A, C, D E, G A

For our purposes all examples in **Template "A"** use the **Minor Pentatonic** scale format over the following chord qualities:

Major 7, Minor 7, 7 Sus 4, Dom 7th (9, 13) and Dom 7 (alt #9, #5)

    (a) **On Minor 7th Chords** — use the Minor Pentatonic scale starting from the **Root, 9th or 5th** of the chord.

    (b) **On Dom 7th (9, 13) or 7 Sus 4 chords** — use Minor Pentatonic scale starting from the **5th, 13th or 9th** of the chord.

    (c) **On Dom 7th (altered #9, #5) chords** — use the Minor Pentatonic scale starting from the **#9 or 7th** of the chord.

    (d) **On Major 7th Chords** — use the Minor Pentatonic scale starting from the **3rd, 7th or 13th** of the chord.

*** Important to note — Starting the pentatonic minor scale from the **root, 3rd, 5th, 7th 9th, #9 or 13th** dependent on the chord types you are playing or hearing automatically implies that the pentatonic scale can start from any one of those positions. However, it doesn't necessarily imply that you have to start your melody making on the first note of the pentatonic scale. For example in **Bar 1** of **Template B**, I delineate the use of **B Minor Pentatonic over Bmin7** to signify that this is the Pentatonic scale I'm using however, I begin my melodic motif on the "7th" because I like the sound of starting on the "A" (I'm still singing B Minor Pentatonic though). Practice this at the piano where it will make the most sense.
[*See Appendix 7 for further clarification*]

11a. Pentatonic Scale-Chord Use

C major Pentatonic uses the same notes as **A minor pentatonic**
For our purposes, all examples will use the minor pentatonic scale format.

1) Use Minor Pentatonic scales on Minor 7th chords:

2) Use Minor Pentatonic scales on Major 7th chords:

3) Use Minor Pentatonic scales on Dominant 7th, specifically 9, 13 chords, or 7sus4 chords:

4) Use Minor Pentatonic scales on Dominant 7th chords, specifically Altered #9, #5 chords:

© Chris McNulty 2017

Exercise 11b — Using Pentatonic Minor over New Day Vamp
(track # 18)

We now take this work into a piece of my own writing. A tune called **New Day**. The excerpt is from the ending vamp.

Template "B" incorporates the following chord progression:

Bmin7 / **C#min7** / **C9 (sus4)** / **D9 (sus4)**.

To allow time to explore the scale and develop melodic motifs each chord is given one measure (on the *New Day* chart each chord is given 2 beats per measure). **Exercises A & B** use the chord progression above. In **Exercise C** to allow for more rhythmic motion, the **C#min** 7 chord has been removed and replaced by an extra bar of **Bmin7**.

In **Exercises A & B** especially, I've kept the melodic and rhythmic motifs simple so you can grasp the method. Once you learn how to hear and choose the correct starting points, create your own melodies and rhythms over these harmonic passages. The "licks" sometimes include notes outside the scale.

*** **Please note**: On **Track 22** (exercise 11b) I've only included the first page — Exercise A and the first 4 bars of Exercise B.

© Chris McNulty 2017

11b. Pentatonic Scale Use
Using Excerpt From Chris' "*NEW DAY*"

Exercise A

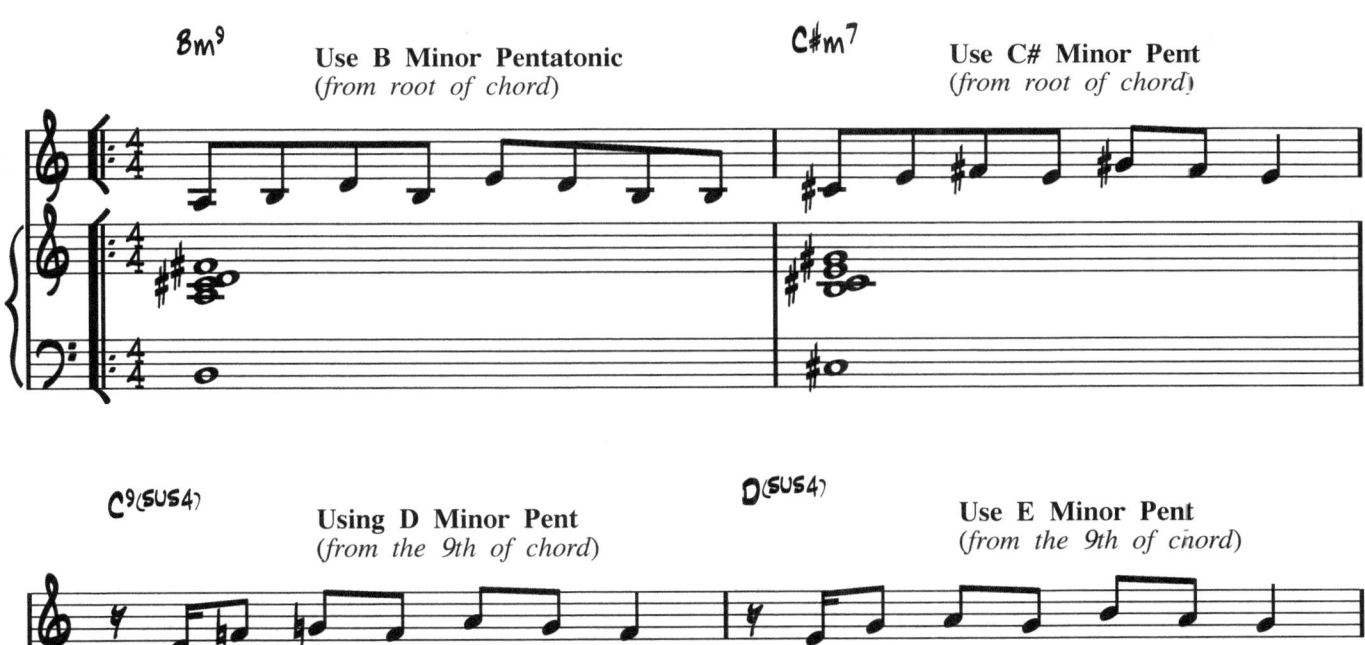

Exercise B — Melody making using chord or tension tones

© Chris McNulty 2017

Melody making using mixed Pentantonics

Exercise C

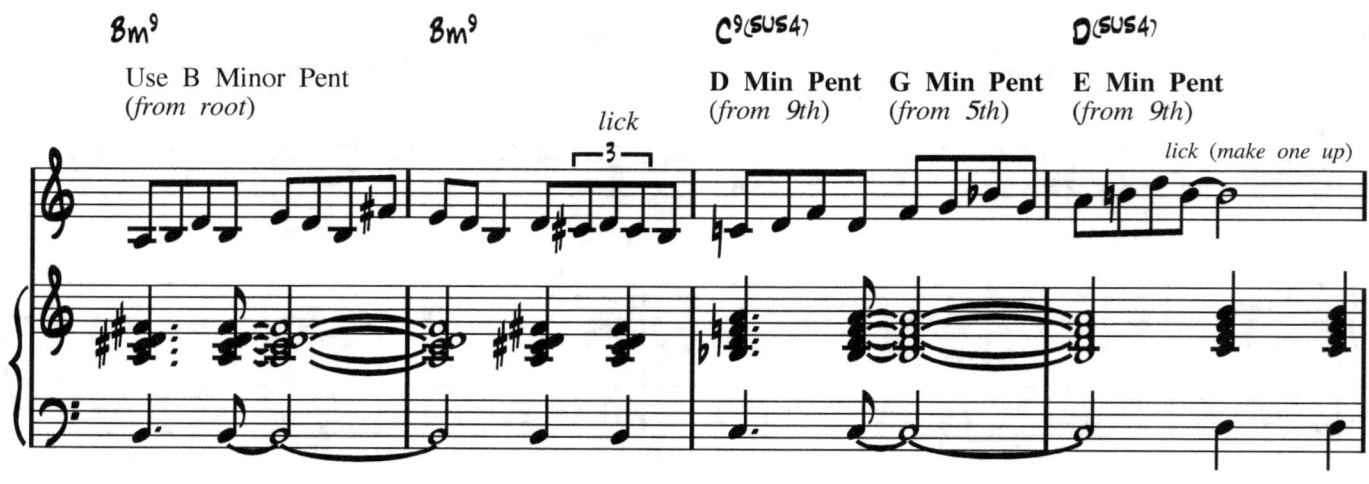

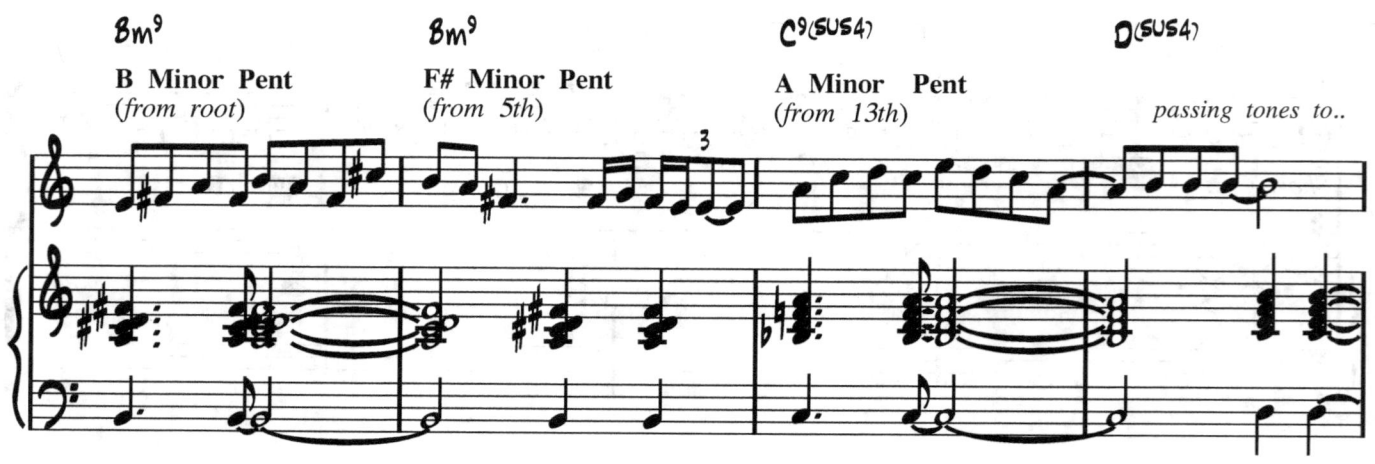

Appendices —

Chord-Scale Source Templates

- 102. Appendix 1. Chord-Scale Tetrachord Structures
- 105. Appendix 2. Chord-Scale Relationships (Parallel & Derivative uses)
- 107. Appendix 3. Types of Dom 7 chord qualities, short cuts and scale choices
- 108. Appendix 4a.b. Common tone-chord/scale relationships
- 111. Appendix 5. Chord voicing short cuts
- 113. Appendix 6. Interchangeable chord options (what you see/what you can play)
- 114. Appendix 7. Pentatonic scale use (Minor/Major)
- 115. Appendix 8a.b. BeBop scale uses (a) chart (b) exercise
- 117. Appendix 9. The Whole Tone scale

Appendix 1
Chord - Scale - Tetrachord Structures

Chord type: Cmaj7(#11)

Scale: C Lydian: 1, 2 (9), 3, #4 (#11), 5, 6 (13), Maj 7, 8

Tetrachords:

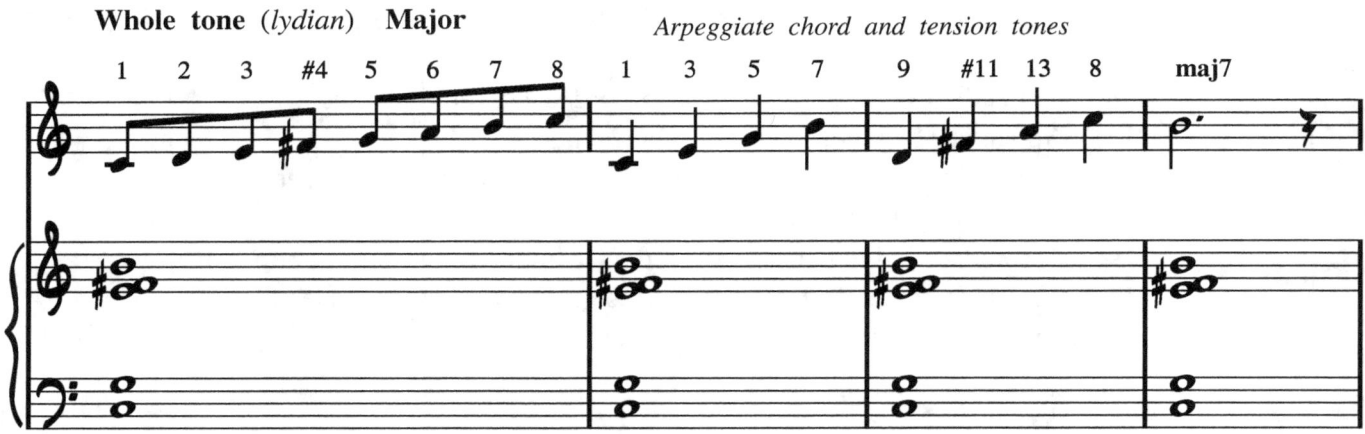

Chord type: Cm7

Scale: C Dorian: 1, 2 (9), b3, 4 (11), 5, 6 (13), b7, 8

Tetrachords:

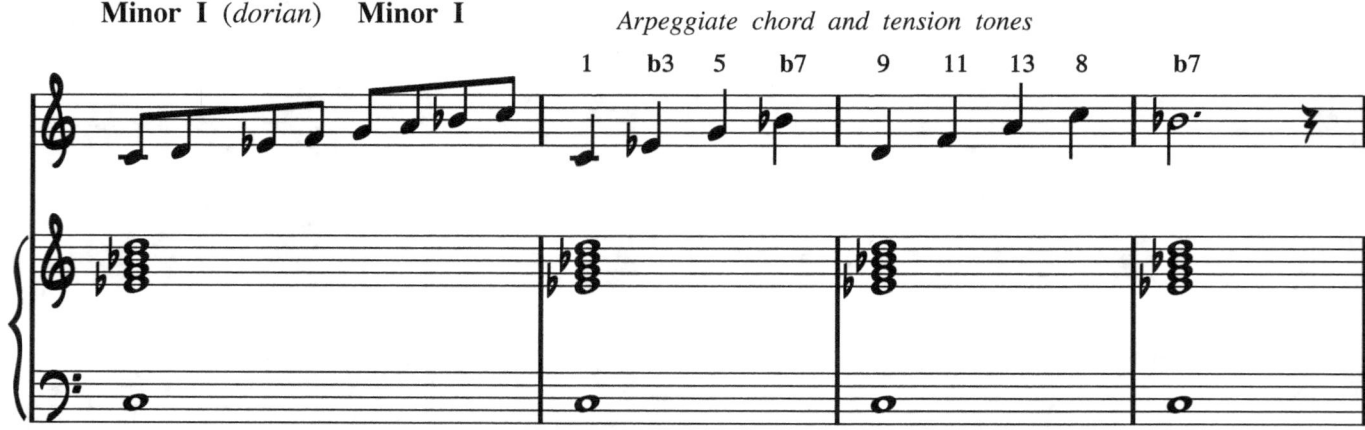

© Chris McNulty 2017

Chord type: Cm7(b5)

Scale: C Locrian (nat 2/9): 1, 2 (9), b3, 4 (11), b5, b6 (b13), b7, 8

Tetrachords:

Type of Chord: C7(9 #11 13)

Scale: C Lydian Dominant: 1, 2 (9), 3, #4 (#11), 5, 6 (13), b7, 8

Tetrachords:

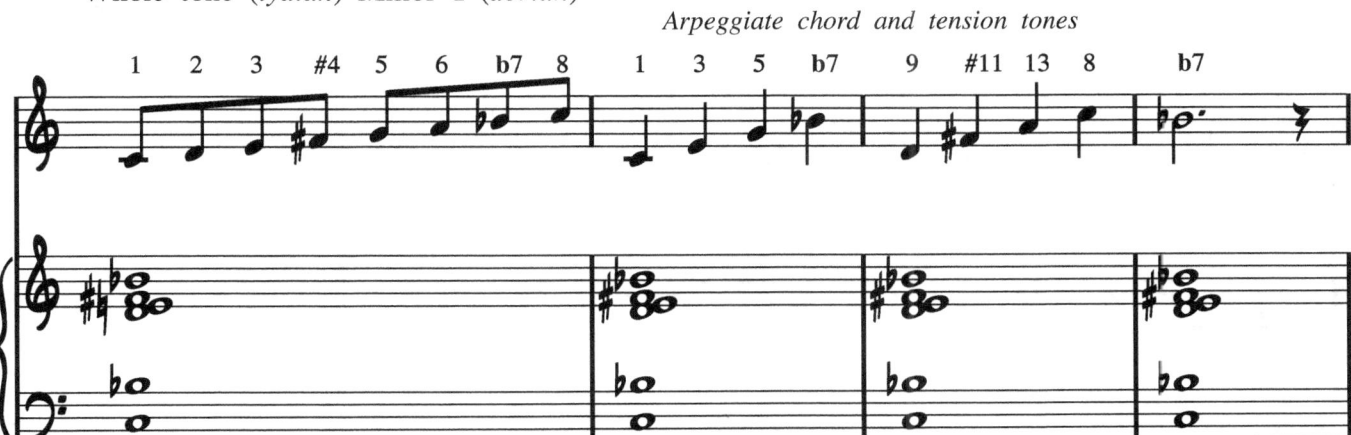

Type of Chord: C+7(#9)

Scale: C Altered: 1 b2 #9 3 #11 b13 b7

Tetrchords:

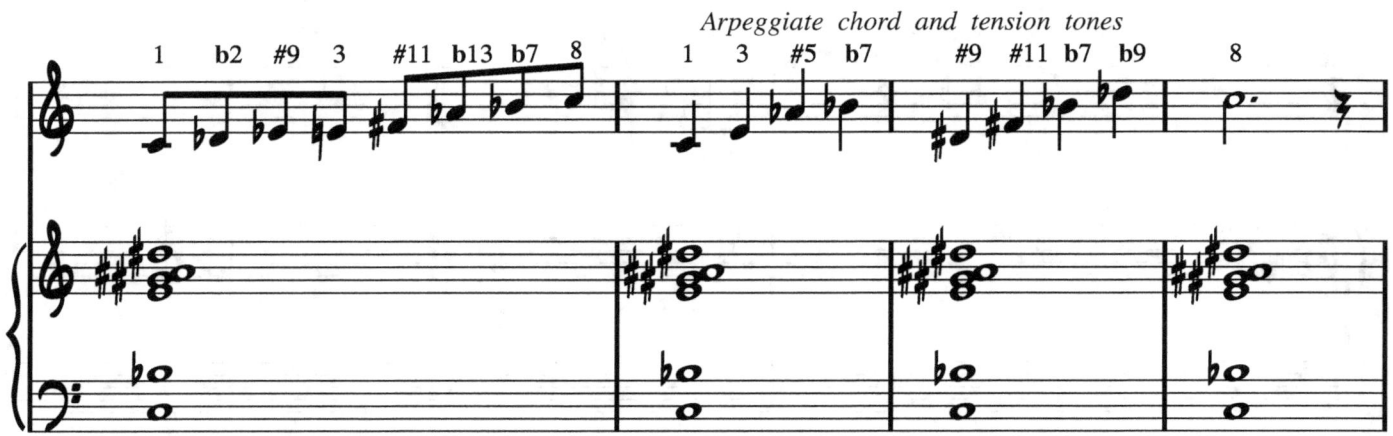

**** Play 1, 3, 5, 7 from each degree/tonality of this scale. They are all Diminished 7 chords

Type of Chord: C7(b9)

Scale: C Diminished (Half-whole): 1, b2 (b9), b3 (#9), 3, #4 (#11), 5, 6 (13), b7, 8

Tetrachords:

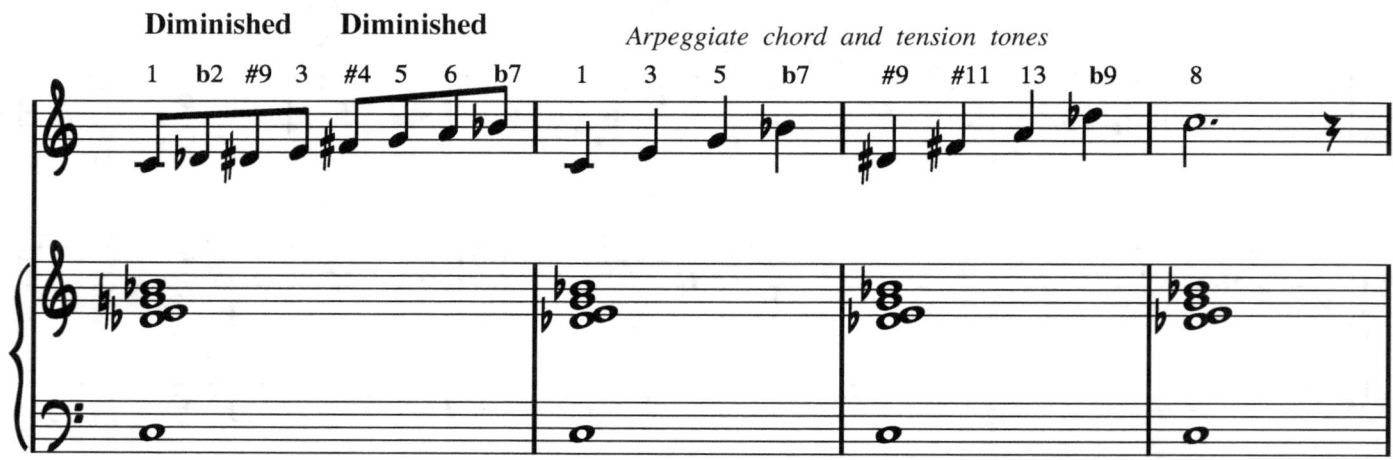

Appendix 2
Chord - Scale Relationships
Parallel & Derivative Use

Parallel - Scale starts from root of chord
Derivative - Scale starts from root of parent scale

Chord	Parallel	Derivative
Maj 7	Ionian (1st mode of major scale)	Play Mixolydian from 5th of chord
Maj 7 #11	Lydian (4th mode of major scale)	Play Locrian (b2) from the #11
Min 7	Dorian (2nd mode of the major scale)	Play Major Scale from the 7th of chord
Maj 7 +5	Lydian Augmented (3rd mode of melodic minor)	Play Melodic Minor from 6th of chord
Min/Maj7	Minor/major (1st mode of melodic minor)	Play Melodic Minor from root of chord (Parallel & Derivative are one and the at 1st degree of scale)
Dom 7 (9, #11, 13)	Lydian Dominant (4th mode of melodic minor)	Play Melodic Minor from 5th of chord
+7, b9, #9, b13	Altered (Diminished/whole tone) (7th mode of melodic minor)	Play melodic minor from b9 (b2) of chord
+7, nat 9, #11	Whole tone	Play C or C# (Db) Whole tone scale based on the root of the chord. **Remember there are only two whole tone scales
Dom 7 (b9, 13)	Diminished (Half-Whole)	Play Half-whole movement from root of chord. **Remember there are only three diminished (half-whole) scales. Each one works over four Dom 7 chords

© Chris McNulty 2017

Chord	Scale	Notes
Dom 7 (b9, b13)	Arabic scale (from root)	Play harmonic minor from 4th of chord **Not derivative in the strictest sense. For example: G7b9, b13 (using C harmonic minor) wouldn't work starting on the note "C" as it would clash with the 3rd of the chord "B".
Sus b9, 13	Phrygian, Nat 6 (2nd mode of melodic minor)	Play melodic minor from 7th of chord (Polychord eg: Eb+maj7/D used modally more than II, V, I)
	**Also a hybrid scale	1, b9, nat 3, 4, 5, 6, b7
1/2 Diminished 7	Locrian (nat 2) (6th mode of melodic minor)	Play Melodic from 3rd of chord
	Locrian (b2) (7th mode of major scale)	Lydian from b5 (#11)
Diminished 7	Diminished (Whole-half)	Play Whole-half movement from root ** Remember there are only three diminished scales. Each work for four chords each

Separate to the above you can use the Minor Pentatonic scale on the following chords played from the notes delineated below:

Chord	Parallel	Derivative
Dom 7 (9, nat 13)	Minor Pentatonic	Played from the 5th, 13th, or 9th
Sus 4 (7)	Minor Pentatonic	Played from the 5th, 13th, or 9th Voice chord: Root (LH) & Maj7 chord from 7th (RH) eg: Bbmaj7/C
Minor 7th	Minor Pentatonic	Played from the root, 9th or 5th
Major 7th	Minor Pentatonic	Played from the 3rd, 6th or 7th

Appendix 3
Types of Dominant 7 Chord Qualities
Scale choices and piano short cuts (using "C" as root)

Chord	Short Cut	Scale Choices
C7 (9, 11)	E-7b5/C	**MIXOLYDIAN** (1, 2, 3, 11, 5, 13, b7) *5th degree of major scale*
C7 (9, #11, 13)	G MinMaj7/C	**LYDIAN DOMINANT** (1, 2, 3, #11, 5, 13, b7) *4th degree of melodic minor* *(Melodic minor played from the 5th of the chord)*
C7 (9, 13)	A Bb D E/C	Use **PENTATONIC MINOR** -3, W, W, -3, W *(played from 5th, 13th, or 9th)*
C7 Sus 4	Bb Maj7/C	Use **PENTATONIC MINOR** -3, W, W, -3, W *(played from 5th, 13th, or 9th)*
C7 Sus b9 13	Db+ Maj 7/C	**PHRYGIAN** Nat 6 (1, b2, b3, 4, 5, 6, b7) *2nd degree of melodic minor* *(Best voicing to use to get the dom7-sus sound: Eb+maj7/D)* *(C melodic minor from 7th of chord, OR use hybrid scale: 1, b2, nat 3, 11, 5, 13, b7)*
C7 (b9, b13)	Dbmin/maj 7/C	**ARABIC SCALE** (1, b2, 3, 4, 5, b13, b7) *5th degree of harmonic minor*
C7 (b9, 13)	Db Dim7/C	**DIMINISHED** (Half-whole) *(Played from root of chord)*
C+7 (b9, #9, b13)	E Bb Eb/C	**ALTERED SCALE** *7th degree of melodic minor* *(Play melodic minor from b2 of chord, OR use pentatonic minor: -3, W, W, -3, W played from #9 or 7th of chord)*

© Chris McNulty 2017

Appendix 4a
Common Tone - Chord Relationships

Half Diminished & Major 7, #11 Chords:

Let's take a look at the relationship between **Half diminished** chords and **Major 7, # 11** chords and see how they relate to each other by finding common tones. Play **C# half diminished (C# minor 7, b5)**. Then play **G Major 7, #11**.

Take a look at the notes that outline each of these chords. Look at the common tones. Now look and listen to how the notes **C#** and **G** are involved in both. The #11 and b5 are key.

Play the chord: **C# 1/2 Diminished (C#min7,b5)** in the left hand (use the sustain pedal). Sing/play **C# Half diminished scale starting from the root (C#)**. Then play the scale from the #11 **(G)** and the scale becomes **G Lydian**. Then play **G Maj 7 #11** in the left hand and play the scale from C# (#11) and the scale becomes Half diminished again. Switch back and forth. Play melodies up and down landing on a note that leads strongly to G major 7, #11 or C# 1/2 Diminished. Now do the same through a cycle of 4th's through all 12 keys….you'll create some beautiful melodies.

Chords with common tonalities from an unrelated key center:

How would we, for instance make sense of seeing **F# 1/2 Diminished** in a piece of music in the **Key of C**? What would we look for?
First look for common tones with **A-7**, which being the **VI chord in C major** has a strong tonic function in the key center. **F# Half Diminished** and **A Minor 6** are basically one and the same chord but with a different root. Perhaps we can make the best sense of how **F# Half Diminished** might work by recognizing its close association tonality wise to the **Key of C** as its relative minor. There are lots of common tones.

Tri-tone Substitutes:

Why they work and how we use them. Play the following progression:
G-7, Db7, C7, F#7, Fmaj7. Look for the common tones. You'll notice that the 3rd's and 7th's are either always involved or a 1/2 step away. The b5 of any V chord shares the same 3rd's and 7th's and is also only a b9 away from the I chord. Try starting on any Minor II chord and follow the same progression.

© Chris McNulty 2017

Note: Learning and memorizing chord changes by Roman Numeral sequence.

Learn in 8 bar sections. Don't try to learn entire songs at one time. Learn a variety of Blues progressions first then go on to for example: "Autumn Leaves," "All The Things You Are" or "I Should Care."

The learning process of understanding harmony is progressive so take your time. Make friends with the piano. It has immeasurable benefits to your development as a jazz singer and is the best tool for learning about jazz harmony. Practice all these exercises at the piano. Try to practice all exercises in as many keys as possible.

Appendix 4b
Common tones - Chord Relationships
Comparing 1/2 Diminished and Major 7, #11 chords

One way of analysing sets of chord changes is by checking out the common tones (notes that are the same).

In the following example check out what notes a Half Diminished chord and a Major 7, #11 chord have in common. Try interchanging the Locrian (b2) scale with the Lydian scale utlizing the tetrachords indicated for each scale.

Chord: Bm7(b5)   Fmaj7(#11)

Scale: Locrian (b2) (*7th mode of the Major scale*)

Tetrachords: **Minor II** (*phrygian*)   **Whole tone** (*lydian*)

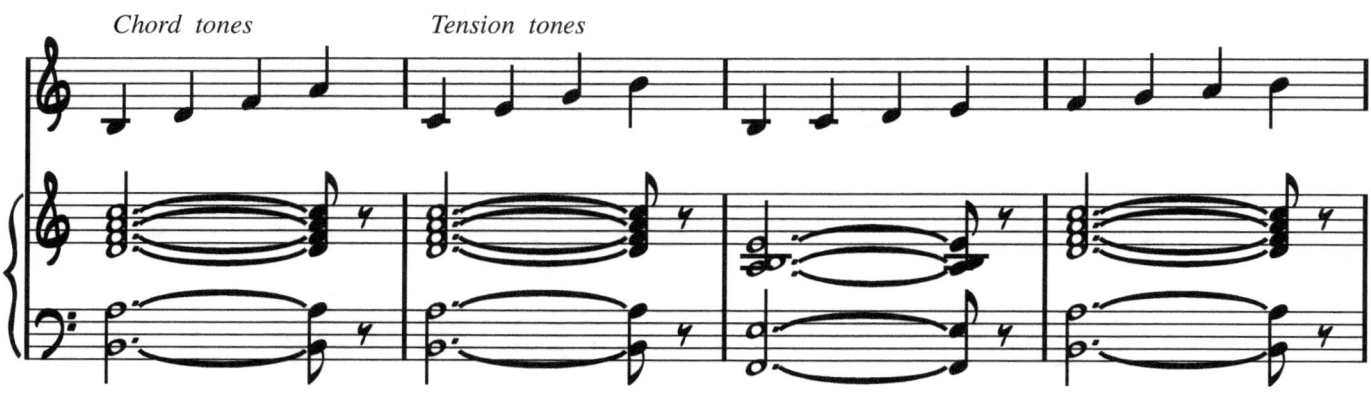

Chord: Fmaj7(#11)   Bm7(b5)

Scale: Lydian (*4th mode of the Major scale*)

Tetrachords: **Whole tone** (*lydian*)   **Major**

© Chris McNulty 2017

Appendix 5
Voicing Short Cuts

Appendix 6
Choice Options for Various Chord Types
(A & B - Interchangeable)

When looking at chord symbols on sheet music it's important to understand that there are many ways to write the same thing. Generally speaking if you see (A) you can play (B).

This list is interchangeable. In other words the reverse is also true. If you see (B) you can also play (A).

(A) What you see	(B) What you can play
Maj 7	Major 9, Maj 6, 6/9, Maj 7 #11
Min 7	Min 9, Min 11, Min 6/9
1/2 Diminished	1/2 Dim (9) OR 1/2 Dim (11), Min 7 no 5th
Diminished 7	Play Dim (min 3rd) with Maj 7
Dom 7	9, #11, 13 (Lydian Dominant)
Augmented/+ Dom 7	#9, #11 (#5 or b13) - Altered
Dom 7 b9	#9, #11, b13, (+5) or Natural 13
Dom 7 sus 4	13 or 9

Appendix 7
The Pentatonic Scale
Minor & Major
5 note scale

C Major Pentatonic and **A Minor Pentatonic** use the same notes

C Major Pentatonic: C, D, E, G, A, C
Scale: **W, W, Minor 3rd, W, Minor 3rd**

A Minor Pentatonic: A, C, D, E, G, A
Scale: **Minor 3rd, W, W, Minor 3rd, W**

Starting from **C** play **Major pentatonic** or
Starting from **A** play **Minor pentatonic** (the intervals are the same)

*** *Use the same principal for all Major and Minor Pentatonic scales*

(a) Use **Minor Pentatonic** on **Dom 7th (9, 13)** or **7 sus 4** chords (starting from the **5th, 13th & 9th** of the chord)

(b) Use **Minor Pentatonic** on **Dom 7th** (altered #9, #5) chords (starting from the **#9, 7th** of the chord)

(c) Use **Minor Pentatonic** on **Minor 7th** chords (starting from **Root, 9th & 5th**)

(d) Use **Minor Pentatonic** on **Major 7th** chords (starting from **6th, 3rd & 7th**)

Appendix 8a
The Be Bop Scale
(8 note scale)

Only use the added chromaticism as part of the Be bop scale, not as part of a melodic construct. For example if you're playing **C7** you can play **Root**, **Maj 7** and **b7** as three consecutive notes but use the Maj 7 as a passing tone only. You would not choose to sit on the Maj 7 on any Dom 7 chord. The same applies to any chromatic passing tone in any scale on other chords listed below. For **C7** play from octave: **(Root, Maj 7, b7, 13)** then use normal scale

(a) **Dom 7** — the **Major 7th** is added (chromatic interval 7-1):
9, 3, 11, 13, b7, Maj7

(b) **Maj 7** — the **Augmented # 5** is added (chromatic interval 5-6):
9, 3, 11, 5, #5, 13, Maj 7

(c) **Min 7** — the **Maj 3rd** is added (chromatic interval 3-4):
9, min 3, maj 3, 11, 5,13 ,b7

Listen to Charlie Parker, Dexter Gordon, Barry Harris (recommend Barry Harris's Chromatic Approach to Harmony), also jazz vocalists Jon Hendricks and Anita Wardell.

8b. BeBop scale uses

Appendix 9
Whole Tone Scale uses

There are only two whole tone scales: **C** and **C#** (Db)

The notes in each scale are as follows:

    C: C, D, E, F#, G# (Ab), Bb, C
    C#:   C#, Eb (D#), F, G, A, B, C#

The key to using the whole tone scale across all 12 keys/chords once again involves looking at and using the scale degrees as the pivot or root note. First look a look at the chord and tension tones. You will notice that they are all a tone apart. Hence the label 'whole tone'. You'll also notice that the 11th (4th) and the 5th are both sharpened. You can also identify this scale as having NO 5th with the 13th (6th) flatted. The 9th is always natural.

The quality of the chord that sources to this scale is always an Augmented 7 nat 9, #11.

"C" whole tone scale works over the following chord quality:
+7 (9, #11) — [Augmented 7, nat 9, #11]

Working from each degree of **C whole tone** scale sing the scale up from each degree accompanied by its related chord (play chord in left hand using sustain pedal) as per the following:

C+7,   D+7,   E+7,   F#+7,   Ab+7,   Bb+7

"C#" whole tone scale works over the following chords (use the exact same principal as above):

C#+7,   Eb+7,   F+7,   G+7,   A+7,   B+7

© Chris McNulty 2017

CD Track listings —

Tracks 1-8, 11, 14, 17, 18 — Piano/Voice.
Tracks 9-10, 12-13 — Trio/Voice

Track 1. Tetrachord template
Track 2. Major scale (**Beginners**)
Track 3. Melodic Minor scale (Min 3, Maj 7th) (**Intermediate**)
Track 4. Harmonic Minor scale (Min 3rd, Min 6th, Maj 7th)
Track 5. Extra Drill over the Altered scale (also known as "the diminished-whole tone" scale) (b9, #9, 3, #11, b13, b7) (7th mode of Melodic Minor)
Track 6. Extra Drill on Arabic Scale (5th mode of Harmonic Minor)
Track 7. Diminished Scale used over Dominant 7 chords (b9, #9, #11, nat13, b7) (use Half-whole motion)
Track 8. Diminished Scale used over Diminished 7 chords (nat 9, min 3rd, b5, b13, major 7) (use Whole-half motion)
Track 9. Singing tetrachords over harmony starting from the same root note (medium bossa nova with Chris)
Track 10. Singing tetrachords over harmony starting from the same root note (medium bossa nova left blank for you to sing)
Track 11. Preparation for singing tetrachords over scales using II, V, I, VI progression.
Track 12. Singing tetrachords over scales using II, V, I, VI progression (slow swing with Chris)
Track 13. Singing tetrachords over scales using II, V, I, VI progression (slow swing blank)
Track 14. Ear warm ups. Preparing for soloing over the changes to "Softly"
Track 15. Using the method over the changes to "Softly" (cascara with Chris)
Track 16. Using the method over the changes to "Softly" (medium swing Chris)
Track 17. Pentatonic scale-chord use template
Track 18. Pentatonic scale use over "New Day" vamp (latin with Chris)

© Chris McNulty 2017

Glossary of terms —

Explanation of terms used throughout this book

Bookends: In this book it refers to the two tetrachords that outline any given scale.

Event: In this book I use it to delineate a chord or system of chords that repeats itself through key changes.

Half-whole motion: A group of notes that move in increments of a semi-tone followed by a whole tone.

Half (1/2) step: A semi-tone. In Western European music a 1/2 step occurs between the notes "B" and "C" and also between the notes "E" and "F"

Harmonic Tetrachord: A 4 note scalar fragment that includes a minor 3rd interval between the flat 9 and the major 3rd. As in: R, b9, Major 3rd, 4th **(C, Db, E, F)**

Measure: The length of any bar in any meter 4/4, 2/4, 3/4, 5/8, 6/8, 7/8, 9/8, 11/8, etc.

Passing chords: A chord that doesn't necessarily belong to the key centre but leads to the next key center usually by a 1/2 step motion (*see Ex 9a.b. - II, V, I, VI*)

Pentatonic Minor: A five (5) note scale that starts with an interval of a minor 3rd followed by two consecutive whole tones, followed by a minor 3rd interval and then a whole tone interval. For example **A Pentatonic Minor** includes the following notes:
A, C, D, E, G, A (also defines a scale that has no 2nd/9th and no 11th/13th).

Pentatonic Major: A five (5) note scale that works in reverse. Starting with two whole tone intervals followed by a minor 3rd, followed by a whole note and then a minor 3rd interval. For example **C Major Pentatonic** includes the same note as A Minor Pentatonic but starts on a different scale degree. The intervals aren't altered, just the starting place: **C, D, E, G, A, C** (also defines scale that has no 4th and no 7th).

Piano short cuts — Slash/chords — Usually the "/" delineates a triad or specific 7 chord played in the RH with the root note played in the LH. For example: **(a) E Maj/C = C Maj 9th**
   (b) Eb Maj7/C = C Minor 9 (I'll Remember April intro).

Root motion: Following the chord movement from the root note of each chord.

Tension tones: The 2nd (9th), 4th (11th), and 6th (13th) notes in a chord

Tetrachords: A four note scalar fragment (makes up part of a scale but is not a scale)
   Whole tone (lydian): A four (4) note scalar fragment that consists of three (3) consecutive whole steps (tones): **C, D, E F#**
   Minor I (dorian): A four note scalar fragment that consists of a whole step, a 1/2 step and whole step: **C, D, Eb F**
   Minor II (phrygian): A four note scalar fragment that consists of a 1/2 step, whole step and whole step: **C, Db, Eb, F**
   Diminished: A four note scalar fragment that consists of a 1/2 step, while step and 1/2 step: **C, Db, Eb, E**
   Major: A four (4) note scalar fragment that consists of a whole step, whole step and 1/2 step: **C, D, E. F**
   Harmonic: A four (4) note scalar fragment that consists of a 1/2 step, a minor 3rd and a 1/2 step: **C, Db, E, F**

Vamp: A set of chord changes (usually two and no more than four) that repeat until cue for ending or sign.

Whole-half motion: Notes with an intervallic pattern of whole tone to semi tone. For example the Diminished (Whole-half) scale

Whole-step: An interval of a whole tone.

Music Fundamentals for Beginners

Augmented (+): Indicates the occurrence of a raised 5th (a 1/2 step up from a perfect 5th)

Bass Clef: The stave below Treble Clef. The notes in the spaces are: **A, C, E, G** (remembered as 'All Cows Eat Grass'). The notes on the lines are: **G, B, D, F, A** (remembered as 'Good Boys Deserve Fruit Always'). Learn them just the way you have the Treble Clef.

Clef: The clef symbol appears at the beginning of every music staff. It tells you which note is found on each line or space.

Chord: An aggregate of musical pitches sounded simultaneously.

Chord progression: A group of chords that connect the harmony of a piece of music/song.

Chord tones: Notes that outline the strong notes in a chord: **Root, 3, 5 & 7**

Diminished: A triad where the 3rd and 5th are flatted. A chord where the 3rd, 5th, 13th are flatted, the 7th is double flatted and there's also a major 7th. The Diminished scale is a 9 note scale. Each chord and tension tone are separated by a minor 3rd interval.

Half Diminished: Delineates the 3rd, 5th and 7th of a 7 chord are flatted.

Harmonic Minor: In western European harmony the Harmonic Minor scale includes a minor 3rd interval which occurs between the flatted 13th and the Major 7th.

Melodic Minor: In western European harmony the Melodic Minor scale includes a flatted 3rd and a major 7th.

Mode: A scale that sources to any degree of a parent scale (from the 1st to the 7th). For example, the Major scale consists of the Ionian, Dorian, Phrygian, Lydian, Mixolydian, Aeolian and Locrian scales. These are all modes of the Major scale.

Roman Numeral (II, V, I) harmony: The Roman numerals (I, II, III, IV,...) denote scale degrees and are used to represent a chord. They denote the root note on which the chord is built. For instance, III denotes the third degree of a scale or the chord built on it. Generally, uppercase Roman numerals (such as I, IV, V) represent major chords while lowercase Roman numerals (such as ii, iii, vi) represent minor chords. Chord formulas are written in Roman numerals to represent the generic form of the progression. Often musicians will learn a piece of music by its chord progression formula. One reason for this is that it is easier to remember since many songs are based on the same or similar formula. Another reason is, it is easier to play a song in different keys if you know the formula.

Root: The first note of a chord/scale.

Scale: Any set of musical notes ordered by fundamental frequency or pitch. A scale ordered by increasing pitch is an ascending scale, and a scale ordered by decreasing pitch is a descending scale.

Scale tone/degree: One of any of the degrees of a scale.

Stave: A staff (or stave) is the name given to the five horizontal lines on which we can write music.

Tonic: The first note of the parent scale or note that delineates the key centre.

Treble Clef: The stave with the first line starting at E above 'Middle C'. The lines are **E, G, B D, F** (Remember 'Every Good Boy Deserves Fruit'). The spaces are: **F, A, C, E** (face)

Triad: A three note chord with a quality of either: major, minor, diminished or Augmented consisting of Root, 3rd and 5th.

www.ingramcontent.com/pod-product-compliance
Lightning Source LLC
Chambersburg PA
CBHW051415070526
44584CB00023B/3441